✝ TIMES ROMAN

Readings, Gospel, Homilies, and Prayers on Advent and Christmas Season

REV. FR. MICHAEL ARBIOL MONSANTO, CSFP

Copyright © 2023 Rev. Fr. Michael Arbiol Monsanto, CSFP

ISBN:
978-1-952874-99-4 (paperback)

All rights reserved. No part of this publication may be reproduced, stored in a retrieval system, or transmitted in any form or by any means - electronic, mechanical, photocopy, recording, scanning, or other – except for brief quotations in critical reviews or articles, without the prior written permission of the publisher.

Published by:

OMNIBOOK CO.
99 Wall Street, Suite 118
New York, NY 10005
USA
+1-866-216-9965
www.omnibook.org

Book purchase: Amazon.com, Barnes & Noble, and www.omnibook.org

Omnibook titles may be purchased in bulk for educational, business, fund-raising, or sales promotional use. For more information please e-mail admin@omnibook.org

TABLE OF CONTENTS

Preface *1*
Opening Prayer *3*
Monday of the First Week of Advent *6*
Tuesday of the First Week of Advent *12*
Wednesday of the First Week of Advent *18*
Thursday of the First Week of Advent *24*
Friday of the First Week of Advent *30*
Saturday of the First Week of Advent *36*
Monday of the Second Week of Advent *42*
Tuesday of the Second Week of Advent *49*
Wednesday of the Second Week of Advent *56*
Thursday of the Second Week of Advent *62*
Friday of the Second Week of Advent *68*
Saturday of the Second Week of Advent *74*
Monday of the Third Week of Advent *80*
Tuesday of the Third Week of Advent *86*
Wednesday of the Third Week of Advent *92*
Thursday of the Third Week in Advent *98*
Friday of the Third Week in Advent *103*
The Weekdays of Advent (December 17) *109*
The Weekdays of Advent (December 18) *116*
The Weekdays of Advent (December 19) *122*
The Weekdays of Advent (December 20) *129*
The Weekdays of Advent (December 21) *135*
The Weekdays of Advent (December 22) *141*
The Weekdays of Advent (December 23) *147*
The Weekdays of Advent (December 24) *153*
Christmas Season (December 26) *159*
Christmas Season (December 27) *165*
Christmas Season (December 28) Feast of the Holy Innocents, martyrs . . . *171*

Christmas Season (December 29) The Fifth Day in the Octave of Christmas 177
Christmas Season (December 30) The Sixth Day in the Octave of Christmas 183
Christmas Season (December 31) The Seventh Day in the Octave of Christmas 189
Weekdays of Christmas Time From January 2 to the Epiphany of the Lord. 195
Christmas Weekday January 3 200
January 4. 206
January 5. 212
January 6. 218
January 7. 225
Or January 7 Monday after Epiphany 231
January 8 Tuesday after Epiphany 236
January 9 Wednesday after Epiphany 242
January 10 Thursday after Epiphany 248
January 11 Friday after Epiphany 254
January 12 Saturday after Epiphany 260
Closing Prayer 266

PREFACE

The seasons of Advent and Christmas invite us to pause, reflect, and embrace the profound mystery of God becoming man. Advent, with its quiet anticipation, beckons us to prepare our hearts and lives for the coming of Christ—not only in the humble manger of Bethlehem but also in the day-to-day moments of our spiritual journey. Christmas, in turn, celebrates the joyful fulfillment of God's promise, as the Word becomes flesh, dwelling among us as the light that dispels the darkness of the world.

This compilation of Readings, Gospel, Reflections and Homilies, and Prayers for the Advent and Christmas Seasons is a spiritual resource for those who seek to journey deeper into the mystery of Christ's incarnation. Through these seasons, we are reminded of God's boundless love, His invitation to reconciliation, and the peace that only His presence can bring to a world often marked by turmoil and strife.

The reflections/homilies in this collection are designed not only to illuminate the Scriptures but also to connect these divine truths with the real experiences of life in our contemporary world. They are written with a pastoral heart, meant to encourage personal transformation and inspire hope in every soul that longs for the Messiah's coming. The prayers included are moments of grace—opportunities to invite the peace, joy, and love of Christ into our hearts, families, and communities.

In a time where materialism and distraction can often overshadow the true meaning of these sacred seasons, this book serves as a reminder of what is truly important: the coming of

Christ, the Prince of Peace, into our world and into our hearts. Whether for personal devotion, spiritual reflection, or ministerial use, may this work lead each reader to a deeper understanding of God's saving plan, manifested through the birth of His Son.

May this humble compilation be a companion through the sacred waiting of Advent and the joyful celebration of Christmas, guiding every soul to encounter the light of Christ in new and profound ways.

REV. FR. MICHAEL ARBIOL MONSANTO, CSFP
Assistant Procurator General
Monastery of the Pilgrim Brothers of St. Francis
Christ the King Sanctuary
Cebu City, Philippines, 6000

OPENING PRAYER

Most Holy Trinity Father, Son and Holy Spirit Triune God, we praise you, we bless you, we adore you, we glorify you, we love you, we give you thanks.

Heavenly Father, Source of all Wisdom and Truth,

As we begin to delve into the sacred Readings, Gospel Homilies, and Prayers that elucidate the profound mysteries of the Advent and Christmas seasons, we humbly ask for Your divine guidance. May Your Holy Spirit enlighten our minds, open our hearts, and fortify our wills, so that the words we read, contemplate, and speak may be imbued with Your grace.

During this Advent season, make us vigilant in preparing the way for Your Son, our Lord Jesus Christ. In the wise words of St. Augustine, "Understanding is the reward of faith. Therefore, seek not to understand that you may believe, but believe that you may understand." Instill in us an unwavering faith, that our understanding may be deepened through these sacred texts and reflections.

As we transition to the Christmas season, let our hearts resound with jubilant praise, recalling the joyous message of the angels to the shepherds on that Holy Night. Illuminate the profound truth of Your incarnation within the readings and homilies, echoing the teachings of St. Thomas Aquinas, who said, "The only-begotten Son of God, wanting to make us sharers in His divinity, assumed our nature, so that He, made Man, might make men gods."

May these readings serve not as mere words on a page but as a living dialogue between the divine and the human. May these homilies be not mere rhetorical exercises but transformative discourses that echo in the corridors of our souls. May these prayers be not rote recitations but heartfelt dialogues with You, our Loving Father.

Through the intercession of the Blessed Virgin Mary, St. Joseph, and all the saints who have walked this earthly pilgrimage in joyful anticipation of the heavenly Jerusalem, may this time of scriptural and theological exploration bring us closer to You, enriching our lives and inspiring us to live according to Your holy will.

We ask all these things in the name of Your Son, our Lord Jesus Christ, who lives and reigns with You and the unity of the Holy Spirit, one God, forever and ever. Amen.

Father, I offer to you the goodness of my heart, the goodness of my soul and the goodness of my whole being. And Father help me to turn my vices into goodness through Christ our Lord our King and our Savior.

Amen.

Opening Prayer

Dear Brothers and Sisters,

You hold in your hands a guide through two of the most spiritually resonant seasons of the Christian liturgical calendar: Advent and Christmas. These seasons, rich in symbolism and deep in theological import, offer a panoramic view of the Christian journey—from expectant waiting to jubilant revelation, from the quiet whisper of hope to the manifestation call of incarnation.

Advent, a season steeped in both penitence and anticipation, calls us to prepare our hearts for the adventus Domini, the coming of the Lord. As the days grow shorter and nature itself seems to hunker down in contemplative quietude, the Church invites us to turn inward, to engage in a spiritual stock-taking. St. Thomas Aquinas reminds us that "to one who has faith, no explanation is necessary. To one without faith, no explanation is possible." Advent bids us to deepen this faith, to reorient ourselves towards the Divine Mystery that seeks to make a dwelling within us.

Christmas, in stark yet harmonious contrast, is a season of exultation, where the celestial rejoices with the terrestrial. In the humble setting of a manger, heaven and earth converge, and the Word becomes flesh. This momentous event is not merely an ancient story but a living reality, continually inviting us to partake in the divine life here and now. It's a testament to God's enduring love for mankind—a love so great that He entered into the very fabric of human history.

Both Advent and Christmas engage us in a dialogue between the divine and the human, the eternal and the temporal. These seasons implore us to examine the state of our souls, to reflect upon the virtues of hope, love, joy, and peace, and to enact them in our daily lives. In a world often marred by uncertainty, these seasons serve as anchors, grounding us in the theological virtues that lead us closer to Christ.

While the seasons may be characterized by distinct moods and themes, they are united in their ultimate purpose: to draw us nearer to the One who is the "Way, the Truth, and the Life." In the words of St. Augustine, "You have made us for yourself, O Lord, and our heart is restless until it rests in you."

As you journey through these sacred times, may you encounter the living God in new and transformative ways. May the readings, Gospel homilies and prayers contained herein guide you to a more profound understanding of the love that God has for each one of us—a love that compels the Divine to draw near to us in the vulnerability of a newborn child. Amen.

MONDAY OF THE FIRST WEEK OF ADVENT

READING 1

Is 2:1-5

This is what Isaiah, son of Amoz,
saw concerning Judah and Jerusalem.

In days to come,
The mountain of the LORD's house
shall be established as the highest mountain
and raised above the hills.
All nations shall stream toward it;
many peoples shall come and say:
"Come, let us climb the LORD's mountain,
to the house of the God of Jacob,
That he may instruct us in his ways,
and we may walk in his paths."
For from Zion shall go forth instruction,
and the word of the LORD from Jerusalem.
He shall judge between the nations,
and impose terms on many peoples.
They shall beat their swords into plowshares
and their spears into pruning hooks;
One nation shall not raise the sword against another,
nor shall they train for war again.

O house of Jacob, come,
let us walk in the light of the LORD!

The word of the Lord.

RESPONSORIAL PSALM

Ps 122:1-2, 3-4b, 4cd-5, 6-7, 8-9

R. Let us go rejoicing to the house of the Lord.

I rejoiced because they said to me,
"We will go up to the house of the LORD."
And now we have set foot
within your gates, O Jerusalem.

R. Let us go rejoicing to the house of the Lord.

Jerusalem, built as a city
with compact unity.
To it the tribes go up,
the tribes of the LORD.

R. Let us go rejoicing to the house of the Lord.

According to the decree for Israel,
to give thanks to the name of the LORD.
In it are set up judgment seats,
seats for the house of David.

R. Let us go rejoicing to the house of the Lord.

Pray for the peace of Jerusalem!
May those who love you prosper!
May peace be within your walls,
prosperity in your buildings.

R. Let us go rejoicing to the house of the Lord.

Because of my relatives and friends
I will say, "Peace be within you!"
Because of the house of the LORD, our God,
I will pray for your good.

R. Let us go rejoicing to the house of the Lord.

ALLELUIA

See Ps 80:4

R. Alleluia, alleluia.
Come and save us, LORD our God;
Let your face shine upon us, that we may be saved.
R. Alleluia, alleluia.

GOSPEL

Mt 8:5-11

When Jesus entered Capernaum,
a centurion approached him and appealed to him, saying,
"Lord, my servant is lying at home paralyzed, suffering dreadfully."
He said to him, "I will come and cure him."
The centurion said in reply,
"Lord, I am not worthy to have you enter under my roof;
only say the word and my servant will be healed.
For I too am a man subject to authority,
with soldiers subject to me.
And I say to one, 'Go,' and he goes;
and to another, 'Come here,' and he comes;
and to my slave, 'Do this,' and he does it."
When Jesus heard this, he was amazed and said to those following him,
"Amen, I say to you, in no one in Israel have I found such faith.
I say to you, many will come from the east and the west,
and will recline with Abraham, Isaac, and Jacob
at the banquet in the Kingdom of heaven."

Brothers and sisters, the Gospel of the Lord.

HOMILY:

In the Gospel of Matthew (8:5-11,) we encounter a Roman centurion with a servant who is gravely ill. This military figure demonstrates a level of faith that leaves even Jesus marveling. The centurion approaches Jesus not with arrogance but with humility, a stark contrast to his role in a society where Roman authority was often brutal and oppressive. He utters the now-immortalized line, "Lord, I am not worthy to have you come under my roof; but only speak the word, and my servant will be healed."

St. Martin of Tours, a soldier turned bishop, who demonstrates a kindred spirit of humility and faith. St. Martin, while still a young officer in the Roman army, encountered a beggar shivering in the cold. Without a second thought, Martin drew his sword and cut his own military cloak in two, giving half to the beggar. That night, he dreamt of Jesus wearing the half-cloak he had given away, affirming his humble act of charity. Here, we see how St. Martin's simple, yet profound, action reflected his deep faith and understanding of Christian charity—paralleling the centurion's unshakeable belief in Christ's authority to heal and transform.

Beloved brothers and sisters in Christ,

As we begin the first week of Advent—a season of preparation and hopeful anticipation—let us reflect on the profound lesson presented by the Roman centurion. It would be easy for us, in these modern times rife with cynicism, to overlook the strength it takes to believe in the way the centurion did. His humility and faith pose a challenge to us: are we equally prepared to acknowledge the authority of Christ in our lives?

The centurion could have easily been dismissive of Christ, rooted as he was in a different tradition and belonging to an occupation that frequently stood in opposition to the teachings of love and peace. Yet, he laid aside all arrogance and pretension, recognizing the omnipotence of Christ. He teaches us that faith and humility are intertwined, and it is this synergy that brings us closer to the divine.

In a world fraught with turmoil and injustice, where authority is often wielded without wisdom or compassion, we ought to remember figures like the centurion and St. Martin of Tours. They show us that true authority stems from a place of love, humility, and an unwavering faith in the power of goodness.

As St. Augustine once said, "Faith is to believe what you do not see; the reward of this faith is to see what you believe." May we, this Advent season, strive to emulate the centurion's unshakable faith and St. Martin's boundless charity, thereby making the journey from merely believing in what we do not see to finally seeing what we have so long believed.

May God bless us all with the grace to live lives rooted in faith, humility, and unconditional love, just as Christ demonstrated and calls us to emulate. Amen.

PRAYER:

Heavenly Father, we come before You on this Monday of the First Week of Advent, our hearts filled with the hope and expectation that this blessed season brings. We reflect on the words and actions of the Roman centurion from the Gospel of Matthew, who in his humble supplication teaches us the true essence of faith and the profound impact of humility.

Lord Jesus, just as the centurion recognized Your divine authority and power to heal, we acknowledge Your sovereignty in our lives. Strengthen our faith so that we may approach You with the same conviction, assured that a single word from You can mend our wounds—physical, emotional, and spiritual. Teach us to say with sincerity, "Lord, I am not worthy to have you come under my roof; but only speak the word, and my servant will be healed."

Holy Spirit, inspire us with the virtues of humility and reverence. May we, like St. Martin of Tours, recognize the face of Christ in the least of our brothers and sisters and extend our cloaks in charity. Lead us to understand that true authority is exercised in service and love, not in dominion or coercion.

As we journey through this Advent season, fill us with anticipatory joy, preparing our hearts to receive the Christ Child anew. May we be inspired by the examples of the saints, drawing us closer to You and fortifying us to live upright and purposeful lives.

We ask for the intercession of our Blessed Mother Mary, who waited in joyful expectation for the birth of her Son. May her prayers guide us as we strive to make room for Jesus in the inn of our hearts.

We offer this prayer in the name of Jesus Christ, our Lord and Savior, who lives and reigns with You and the unity of the Holy Spirit, one God, forever and ever. Amen.

TUESDAY OF THE FIRST WEEK OF ADVENT

READING 1

Is 11:1-10

On that day,
A shoot shall sprout from the stump of Jesse,
and from his roots a bud shall blossom.
The Spirit of the LORD shall rest upon him:
a Spirit of wisdom and of understanding,
A Spirit of counsel and of strength,
a Spirit of knowledge and of fear of the LORD,
and his delight shall be the fear of the LORD.
Not by appearance shall he judge,
nor by hearsay shall he decide,
But he shall judge the poor with justice,
and decide aright for the land's afflicted.
He shall strike the ruthless with the rod of his mouth,
and with the breath of his lips he shall slay the wicked.
Justice shall be the band around his waist,
and faithfulness a belt upon his hips.

Then the wolf shall be a guest of the lamb,
and the leopard shall lie down with the kid;
The calf and the young lion shall browse together,
with a little child to guide them.
The cow and the bear shall be neighbors,
together their young shall rest;
the lion shall eat hay like the ox.
The baby shall play by the cobra's den,
and the child lay his hand on the adder's lair.
There shall be no harm or ruin on all my holy mountain;
for the earth shall be filled with knowledge of the LORD,
as water covers the sea.

On that day,
The root of Jesse,
set up as a signal for the nations,
The Gentiles shall seek out,
for his dwelling shall be glorious.

The word of the Lord.

RESPONSORIAL PSALM

Ps 72:1-2, 7-8, 12-13, 17

R. (see 7) Justice shall flourish in his time, and fullness of peace forever.
O God, with your judgment endow the king,
and with your justice, the king's son;
He shall govern your people with justice
and your afflicted ones with judgment.

R. Justice shall flourish in his time, and fullness of peace forever.

Justice shall flower in his days,
and profound peace, till the moon be no more.
May he rule from sea to sea,
and from the River to the ends of the earth.

R. Justice shall flourish in his time, and fullness of peace forever.
He shall rescue the poor when he cries out,
and the afflicted when he has no one to help him.
He shall have pity for the lowly and the poor;
the lives of the poor he shall save.
R. Justice shall flourish in his time, and fullness of peace forever.
May his name be blessed forever;
as long as the sun his name shall remain.
In him shall all the tribes of the earth be blessed;
all the nations shall proclaim his happiness.

R. Justice shall flourish in his time, and fullness of peace forever.

ALLELUIA

R. Alleluia, alleluia.

Behold, our Lord shall come with power;
he will enlighten the eyes of his servants.
R. Alleluia, alleluia.

GOSPEL

Lk 10:21-24

Jesus rejoiced in the Holy Spirit and said,
"I give you praise, Father, Lord of heaven and earth,
for although you have hidden these things
from the wise and the learned
you have revealed them to the childlike.
Yes, Father, such has been your gracious will.
All things have been handed over to me by my Father.
No one knows who the Son is except the Father,
and who the Father is except the Son
and anyone to whom the Son wishes to reveal him."

Turning to the disciples in private he said,
"Blessed are the eyes that see what you see.
For I say to you,
many prophets and kings desired to see what you see,
but did not see it,
and to hear what you hear, but did not hear it."

Brothers and sisters, the Gospel of the Lord.

HOMILY:

As we contemplate the Gospel of Luke (10:21-24,) where Jesus praises God for revealing truths to "little ones" rather than the wise and learned, we might recall the story of St. Thérèse of Lisieux. Known for her "Little Way," St. Thérèse epitomized the Gospel's message. She wasn't a theologian or a scholar but a Carmelite nun who died at the young age of 24. She embraced her littleness, her simplicity, and she found joy in everyday duties and small sacrifices. It was through this humble approach that she came to a profound understanding of God's love and mercy. Even Pope Pius X referred to her as "the greatest saint of modern times," acknowledging that her simplicity revealed a deep spiritual wisdom.

Dearly beloved in Christ,

As we gather on this Tuesday of the first week of Advent, we are presented with a Gospel that speaks of the joy and wisdom found in humility and simplicity. In the Gospel of Luke, our Lord Jesus offers a prayer of thanksgiving, extolling the Father for the divine wisdom granted not to the wise and learned of this world, but to the "little ones."

Jesus reminds us that the kingdom of God is not an exclusive club for the intellectually elite or morally superior. Rather, it is a divine gift, freely offered to all who approach with the heart of a child—open, trusting, and humble. To be childlike is not to be naive or foolish; it is to possess a purity of heart that allows us to see God as He truly is.

In a world that often equates sophistication with wisdom and complexity with depth, the Gospel today challenges us to think otherwise. We are called to embody humility, acknowledging that no amount of human knowledge can replace divine wisdom. It is a wisdom so profound that even the angels long to comprehend it, yet so simple that it is grasped by the humble and the meek.

St. Augustine said, "Unless you believe, you will not understand." He reminds us that the first step to gaining spiritual wisdom is faith—a faith that is unpretentious, trusting, and complete. St. Thérèse of Lisieux, in her Little Way, illustrates how grand truths often reside in simple faith.

As we continue our Advent journey, let us strive to become the "little ones" Jesus speaks of: simple yet profound, humble yet wise. In doing so, we open ourselves to the richness of God's revelation—a revelation that transforms our lives and prepares us to welcome the Christ Child with joy and wonder.

May we all be blessed with the wisdom of the "little ones," understanding the mysteries of God through the lens of humility and simplicity, and thereby preparing our hearts to fully receive the coming of our Lord. Amen.

PRAYER:

Almighty God, we come before Your presence this Tuesday of the first week of Advent, with hearts aspiring to be like the "little ones" described in today's Gospel from Luke. We hear the joyful thanksgiving in Jesus' words as He praises You for revealing divine truths not to the wise and learned, but to those with hearts open like children.

Lord Jesus, help us to attain this blessed simplicity and humility. Open our hearts to Your message, and allow us to find delight in the divine wisdom often hidden in plain sight. Like St. Thérèse of Lisieux, may we embrace the "Little Way," understanding that in the simplicity of our daily lives, we find the path to true wisdom and closer union with You.

Holy Spirit, guardian of all truth, guide us to the wisdom that transcends human knowledge and understanding. In a world that often values skepticism and complexity, help us to appreciate the profound yet simple truths that bring us closer to the essence of divinity.

During this season of Advent, as we await the incarnation of Wisdom itself in the form of a vulnerable child, fill our hearts with humility. Help us to empty ourselves of pride and self-importance, making room for the virtues of faith, hope, and charity.

We ask for the intercession of the Blessed Virgin Mary, who in her humble acceptance of Your will, became the Mother of Wisdom incarnate. May her prayers guide us as we navigate the path to becoming recipients of Your eternal wisdom.

In a spirit of anticipatory joy and gratitude, we offer this prayer in the name of Your Son, Jesus Christ, who is the source of all wisdom and who lives and reigns with You and the unity of the Holy Spirit, one God, forever and ever. Amen.

WEDNESDAY OF THE FIRST WEEK OF ADVENT

READING 1

Is 25:6-10a

On this mountain the LORD of hosts
will provide for all peoples
A feast of rich food and choice wines,
juicy, rich food and pure, choice wines.
On this mountain he will destroy
the veil that veils all peoples,
The web that is woven over all nations;
he will destroy death forever.
The Lord GOD will wipe away
the tears from all faces;
The reproach of his people he will remove
from the whole earth; for the LORD has spoken.

On that day it will be said:
"Behold our God, to whom we looked to save us!
This is the LORD for whom we looked;
let us rejoice and be glad that he has saved us!"
For the hand of the LORD will rest on this mountain.

The word of the Lord.

RESPONSORIAL PSALM

Ps 23:1-3a, 3b-4, 5, 6

R. (6cd) I shall live in the house of the Lord all the days of my life.
The LORD is my shepherd; I shall not want.
In verdant pastures he gives me repose;
Beside restful waters he leads me;
he refreshes my soul.

R. I shall live in the house of the Lord all the days of my life.

He guides me in right paths
for his name's sake.
Even though I walk in the dark valley
I fear no evil; for you are at my side
With your rod and your staff
that give me courage.

R. I shall live in the house of the Lord all the days of my life.

You spread the table before me
in the sight of my foes;
You anoint my head with oil;
my cup overflows.

R. I shall live in the house of the Lord all the days of my life.

Only goodness and kindness follow me
all the days of my life;
And I shall dwell in the house of the LORD
for years to come.

R. I shall live in the house of the Lord all the days of my life.

ALLELUIA

R. Alleluia, alleluia.
Behold, the Lord comes to save his people;
blessed are those prepared to meet him.
R. Alleluia, alleluia.

GOSPEL

Mt 15:29-37

At that time:
Jesus walked by the Sea of Galilee,
went up on the mountain, and sat down there.
Great crowds came to him,
having with them the lame, the blind, the deformed, the mute,
and many others.
They placed them at his feet, and he cured them.
The crowds were amazed when they saw the mute speaking,
the deformed made whole,
the lame walking,
and the blind able to see,
and they glorified the God of Israel.

Jesus summoned his disciples and said,
"My heart is moved with pity for the crowd,
for they have been with me now for three days
and have nothing to eat.
I do not want to send them away hungry,
for fear they may collapse on the way."
The disciples said to him,
"Where could we ever get enough bread in this deserted place
to satisfy such a crowd?"
Jesus said to them, "How many loaves do you have?"
"Seven," they replied, "and a few fish."
He ordered the crowd to sit down on the ground.
Then he took the seven loaves and the fish,
gave thanks, broke the loaves,
and gave them to the disciples, who in turn gave them to the crowds.
They all ate and were satisfied.
They picked up the fragments left over–seven baskets full.

Brothers and sisters, the Gospel of the Lord.

HOMILY:

To illuminate the Gospel of Matthew (15:29-37,) where Jesus performs miracles of healing and feeds a multitude with seven loaves of bread and a few fish, let us recall the life of St. Elizabeth of Hungary. Known for her devotion to the poor, St. Elizabeth was once stopped by her husband, Ludwig, on her way to distribute bread to the needy. Skeptical, he demanded to see what was hidden in her cloak. Miraculously, when she opened her cloak, roses fell out instead of bread. This story reflects how divine providence works through those who give unselfishly. Like Christ, St. Elizabeth gave not just material sustenance but hope and dignity to the marginalized.

Dear brothers and sisters in Christ,

We are blessed on this Wednesday of the First Week of Advent to hear from the Gospel of Matthew a compelling account of Jesus' healing and miraculous feeding of a great crowd. These acts are not simply isolated miracles; they speak of a much deeper reality that intersects profoundly with our own spiritual journeys.

At first glance, the events appear to concern physical healing and hunger. However, on a deeper level, they address the spiritual malaise that afflicts humanity. How often do we, too, find ourselves famished in spirit, longing for meaning and wholeness? How often do we suffer from the maladies of the soul—doubt, despair, loneliness?

In today's Gospel, Jesus demonstrates that He is not just concerned with our physical well-being, but profoundly invested in our spiritual health. He offers a holistic healing, addressing the needs of both body and soul. He nourishes not just with bread and fish, but with hope, compassion, and love.

The Gospel also raises the theme of divine providence. Jesus, with just seven loaves and a few fish, feeds the multitude. This act serves as a reminder that God's grace is abundant, overflowing, and available to all who seek it. St. Elizabeth of Hungary, through her own acts of compassion, mirrored this boundless grace in her devotion to the needy.

St. Augustine reminds us that "God is always trying to give good things to us, but our hands are too full to receive them." This Advent season provides a prime opportunity for us to empty our hands of worldly distractions and open our hearts to the limitless grace God wishes to pour into our lives.

As we journey through this blessed season of Advent, let us be inspired by the examples of Christ, the saints, and the philosophers who understood that true fulfillment and wisdom are found in a life oriented towards divine love and human compassion. Let us aim to be instruments of God's miraculous provision, feeding the hungry in our midst—not just with material sustenance but with the Bread of Life, the source of eternal joy and peace. Amen.

PRAYER:

Almighty God, we approach Your throne of grace this Wednesday of the First Week of Advent with humble hearts, mindful of Your compassion and boundless love. Today's Gospel from Matthew reveals Your desire to nourish and heal, to restore and renew both body and soul.

Lord Jesus Christ, You who healed the sick and fed the hungry, instill within us a keen awareness of those who are physically and spiritually in need. May we be Your hands and feet on earth, bringing relief to those who suffer and nourishment to those who hunger for justice, love, and understanding.

Holy Spirit, fill us with the courage to step out in faith, trusting in Your divine providence, just as the crowd in today's Gospel trusted in Jesus. Remind us that when resources seem scant and problems overwhelming, Your grace is sufficient for all our needs. May we, like St. Elizabeth of Hungary, be faithful stewards of the blessings we receive, always seeking to share them in acts of charity and kindness.

As we traverse the sacred season of Advent, prepare our hearts to receive the Christ Child anew, in whom all our hopes and fears are met. Grant us the wisdom to understand that the birth of Jesus is not just a historical event but a continual reality, taking place whenever love, peace, and joy are made manifest among us.

We look to the Blessed Virgin Mary, a model of perfect obedience and trust, asking for her prayers as we strive to live lives of service and devotion.

In this time of expectant waiting, we offer this prayer in the name of Your Son, Jesus Christ, who came to heal, to feed, and to save, and who lives and reigns with You and unity of the Holy Spirit, one God, forever and ever. Amen.

THURSDAY OF THE FIRST WEEK OF ADVENT

READING 1

Is 26:1-6

On that day they will sing this song in the land of Judah:

"A strong city have we;
he sets up walls and ramparts to protect us.
Open up the gates
to let in a nation that is just,
one that keeps faith.
A nation of firm purpose you keep in peace;
in peace, for its trust in you."

Trust in the LORD forever!
For the LORD is an eternal Rock.
He humbles those in high places,
and the lofty city he brings down;
He tumbles it to the ground,
levels it with the dust.
It is trampled underfoot by the needy,
by the footsteps of the poor.

The word of the Lord.

RESPONSORIAL PSALM

Ps 118:1 and 8-9, 19-21, 25-27a

R. (26a) Blessed is he who comes in the name of the Lord.
or:
R. Alleluia.

Give thanks to the LORD, for he is good,
for his mercy endures forever.
It is better to take refuge in the LORD
than to trust in man.
It is better to take refuge in the LORD
than to trust in princes.

R. Blessed is he who comes in the name of the Lord.
or:
R. Alleluia.

Open to me the gates of justice;
I will enter them and give thanks to the LORD.
This gate is the LORD's;
the just shall enter it.
I will give thanks to you, for you have answered me
and have been my savior.

R. Blessed is he who comes in the name of the Lord.
or:
R. Alleluia.

O LORD, grant salvation!
O LORD, grant prosperity!
Blessed is he who comes in the name of the LORD;
we bless you from the house of the LORD.
The LORD is God, and he has given us light.

R. Blessed is he who comes in the name of the Lord.
or:
R. Alleluia.

ALLELUIA

Is 55:6

R. Alleluia, alleluia.
Seek the LORD while he may be found;
call him while he is near.
R. Alleluia, alleluia.

GOSPEL

Mt 7:21, 24-27

Jesus said to his disciples:
"Not everyone who says to me, 'Lord, Lord,'
will enter the Kingdom of heaven,
but only the one who does the will of my Father in heaven.

"Everyone who listens to these words of mine and acts on them
will be like a wise man who built his house on rock.
The rain fell, the floods came,
and the winds blew and buffeted the house.
But it did not collapse; it had been set solidly on rock.
And everyone who listens to these words of mine
but does not act on them
will be like a fool who built his house on sand.
The rain fell, the floods came,
and the winds blew and buffeted the house.
And it collapsed and was completely ruined."

Brothers and sisters, the Gospel of the Lord.

HOMILY:

Today's Gospel of Matthew (7:21, 24-27,) warns us about the importance of building our lives on a solid foundation, let us reflect upon the life of St. Augustine of Hippo. A brilliant thinker, he initially sought to build his life on worldly pleasures and intellectual pursuits. It wasn't until he heard the teachings of St. Ambrose and read the Scriptures that he realized his life was like a house built on sand. He famously uttered, "You have made us for yourself, O Lord, and our hearts are restless until they rest in you." Only then did St. Augustine start to build his life on the rock of faith, going on to become one of Christianity's most influential theologians.

Beloved in Christ,

As we gather on this Thursday of the First Week of Advent, the Gospel from Matthew presents us with a timeless teaching about the foundation upon which we should build our lives. Christ declares, "Everyone who listens to these words of mine and acts on them will be like a wise man who built his house on rock."

This message from our Lord carries an urgency as we navigate our modern world, which is fraught with fleeting distractions and shaky foundations. The Gospel prompts us to examine the quality of our spiritual structures. Are they built on the rock of genuine faith and virtuous deeds, or are they precariously perched upon the sands of empty words and transient desires?

St. Augustine provides a compelling example of this transformation. He realized that earthly wisdom, no matter how sophisticated, cannot serve as the ultimate foundation for a meaningful life. It is a reminder that even the most brilliant minds are susceptible to building houses on sand if they rely solely on human reasoning and neglect divine wisdom.

The Gospel challenges us to ensure that our lives are firmly grounded in the teachings of Christ, which stand as the bedrock of true wisdom and ultimate purpose. However, it is not enough to simply listen to these teachings; we must act upon them. As St. James tells us, "Be doers of the word, and not hearers only, deceiving yourselves" (James 1:22).

This Advent season is a sacred time for reevaluation and spiritual realignment. Let it serve as a workshop where we reassess the durability of our spiritual edifices, fortifying the weak spots and laying down new stones of prayer, penance, and almsgiving.

As we prepare for the coming of the Christ Child, let us heed the wisdom of the saints who have walked before us. Let their lives be our guiding lights, illuminating the path towards a life that is not merely structurally sound but eternally significant. Let us be builders, not just of worldly success but of heavenly treasure. Amen.

PRAYER:

Eternal God, on this Thursday of the First Week of Advent, we humbly approach Your presence, bearing in our hearts the solemn words of today's Gospel from Matthew: the admonition to build our lives on solid foundations. We recognize that the mere utterance of faith is not sufficient; true faith is borne out in action, in building a life on the rock of Your word.

Lord Jesus, You are that rock. Guide us to build our lives not on the shifting sands of worldly desires, material success, or intellectual vanity, but on Your teachings and example. Grant us the grace to not only be listeners but doers of Your word, committed to translating Your teachings into concrete actions that reflect Your love and justice.

Holy Spirit, inspire us with the wisdom and courage we need to examine our lives critically. Where our foundation is weak, fortify us. Where it is broken, restore us. May our souls be like well-constructed edifices, built on faith, upheld by hope, and inhabited by love.

St. Augustine, a sinner turned saint, found peace only when he built his life on the cornerstone of Christ. His journey is a testament to the transformative power of divine grace and wisdom. We seek his intercession as we strive to align our lives with the eternal truths of the Gospel.

As we journey through Advent, prepare our hearts and minds to receive anew the Christ Child, who is the visible sign of Your invisible grace and the eternal Word made flesh. May His coming be for us the laying of the cornerstone around which the structure of our lives takes shape and meaning.

In a spirit of hopeful expectation and deepening faith, we offer this prayer through Jesus Christ, Your Son, who is the Way, the Truth, and the Life, and who lives and reigns with You and the unity of the Holy Spirit, one God, forever and ever. Amen.

FRIDAY OF THE FIRST WEEK OF ADVENT

READING 1

IS 29:17-24

Thus says the Lord GOD:
But a very little while,
and Lebanon shall be changed into an orchard,
and the orchard be regarded as a forest!
On that day the deaf shall hear the words of a book;
And out of gloom and darkness,
the eyes of the blind shall see.
The lowly will ever find joy in the LORD,
and the poor rejoice in the Holy One of Israel.
For the tyrant will be no more
and the arrogant will have gone;
All who are alert to do evil will be cut off,
those whose mere word condemns a man,
Who ensnare his defender at the gate,
and leave the just man with an empty claim.
Therefore thus says the LORD,
the God of the house of Jacob,
who redeemed Abraham:
Now Jacob shall have nothing to be ashamed of,
nor shall his face grow pale.
When his children see
the work of my hands in his midst,
They shall keep my name holy;
they shall reverence the Holy One of Jacob,
and be in awe of the God of Israel.
Those who err in spirit shall acquire understanding,
and those who find fault shall receive instruction.

The word of the Lord.

RESPONSORIAL PSALM

PS 27:1, 4, 13-14

R. (1a) The Lord is my light and my salvation.

The LORD is my light and my salvation;
whom should I fear?
The LORD is my life's refuge;
 of whom should I be afraid?

R. The Lord is my light and my salvation.

One thing I ask of the LORD;
this I seek:
To dwell in the house of the LORD
all the days of my life,
That I may gaze on the loveliness of the LORD
and contemplate his temple.

R. The Lord is my light and my salvation.

I believe that I shall see the bounty of the LORD
in the land of the living.
Wait for the LORD with courage;
be stouthearted, and wait for the LORD.

R. The Lord is my light and my salvation.

ALLELUIA

R. Alleluia, alleluia.
Behold, our Lord shall come with power;
he will enlighten the eyes of his servants.
R. Alleluia, alleluia.

GOSPEL

MT 9:27-31

As Jesus passed by, two blind men followed him, crying out,
"Son of David, have pity on us!"
When he entered the house,
the blind men approached him and Jesus said to them,
"Do you believe that I can do this?"
"Yes, Lord," they said to him.
Then he touched their eyes and said,
"Let it be done for you according to your faith."
And their eyes were opened.
Jesus warned them sternly,
"See that no one knows about this."
But they went out and spread word of him through all that land.

Brothers and sisters, the Gospel of the Lord.

HOMILY:

To understand the depth of today's Gospel from Matthew (9:27-31,) where Jesus heals two blind men, we might consider the life of St. Lucy, whose name means 'light.' St. Lucy was a young Christian martyr who is often invoked for ailments of the eyes. According to tradition, she gave away her dowry to the poor, signifying her spiritual sight in recognizing the true treasure in heaven over worldly riches. Her life serves as an example of the 'spiritual sight' that we all need to navigate through the darkness of this world.

Beloved brothers and sisters,

As we come together on this Friday of the First Week of Advent, we are graced with a Gospel passage from Matthew that speaks to the transformative power of faith. Two blind men call out to Jesus, addressing Him as "Son of David," and they are healed because of their faith.

The story is not merely a tale of physical healing; it encapsulates the broader narrative of spiritual blindness, a condition afflicting many in today's world. In our modern society, replete with distractions and superficial allurements, it is easy to lose sight of what is genuinely important. Spiritual blindness can manifest in our failure to recognize God's presence in our lives, in our indifference to the suffering of our neighbors, or in our pursuit of material rather than heavenly riches.

St. Lucy, whose life story stands as an icon of spiritual sight, challenges us to reassess our priorities. By forsaking her worldly dowry for the betterment of the poor, she teaches us that true sight extends beyond the physical and penetrates to the essence of life—our relationship with God and with each other.

What are we blind to in our lives? Are we missing the presence of God in the daily occurrences that we often take for granted? Are we oblivious to the opportunities to manifest Christ's love to those around us? The blind men in the Gospel were physically incapable of seeing, yet they had the 'spiritual sight' to recognize Jesus as the "Son of David." How much more then should we, who have been gifted with both physical and spiritual vision, strive to see the face of Christ in our lives and in the world around us?

As philosopher Søren Kierkegaard profoundly noted, "Faith sees best in the dark." In this season of Advent, a season of hopeful anticipation yet also a season that calls us to introspection and repentance, let us strive to shed our spiritual blindness. Let us invite the divine physician to heal our eyes, that we may see the world and ourselves as God sees—imbued with the potential for love, grace, and transformation.

In our journey through this sacred season, may we be like the blind men—desperate for Jesus, aware of our deficiencies, yet full of faith that He can, and will, heal and complete us. Amen.

PRAYER:

Heavenly Father, we gather here on this Friday of the First Week of Advent with hearts turned towards You, reflecting on the poignant Gospel message from Matthew. In it, two blind men cry out to Jesus, the "Son of David," for healing, and their sight is miraculously restored by their faith.

Lord, in a world that often seems shrouded in darkness, both literal and metaphorical, we beseech You to grant us the grace of spiritual sight. We are aware that many forms of blindness afflict us—not just physical but also moral and spiritual. Enlighten the eyes of our heart, that we may discern Your will in our lives, recognize the dignity in our fellow human beings, and perceive Your divine hand in creation.

Jesus Christ, Divine Physician, You opened the eyes of the blind and made the lame walk. We earnestly ask that You also touch our lives and heal the blindness that prevents us from seeing the fullness of Your glory. Let our faith be like that of the blind men, unwavering and fully reliant on Your boundless mercy and power.

Holy Spirit, guide us to live out our faith in concrete ways, especially during this Advent season as we prepare to celebrate the incarnation of our Savior. Help us to witness to others the light of Christ, which dispels the darkness and brings hope to the world.

In this season of preparation and waiting, we invoke the intercession of St. Lucy, whose name signifies light and who, with her very life, illuminated the path of spiritual wisdom. May her example inspire us to relinquish worldly attachments and seek the true Light of the World.

Father, Your advent is near. Prepare our hearts to welcome You anew, that come Christmas, we might behold Your glory with newly restored vision—seeing not just with our eyes, but understanding with our hearts.

We offer this prayer through Your Son, Jesus Christ, who lives and reigns with You and the unity of the Holy Spirit, one God, forever and ever. Amen.

SATURDAY OF THE FIRST WEEK OF ADVENT

READING 1

Is 30:19-21, 23-26

Thus says the Lord GOD,
the Holy One of Israel:
O people of Zion, who dwell in Jerusalem,
no more will you weep;
He will be gracious to you when you cry out,
as soon as he hears he will answer you.
The Lord will give you the bread you need
and the water for which you thirst.
No longer will your Teacher hide himself,
but with your own eyes you shall see your Teacher,
While from behind, a voice shall sound in your ears:
"This is the way; walk in it,"
when you would turn to the right or to the left.

He will give rain for the seed
that you sow in the ground,
And the wheat that the soil produces
will be rich and abundant.
On that day your flock will be given pasture
and the lamb will graze in spacious meadows;
The oxen and the asses that till the ground
will eat silage tossed to them
with shovel and pitchfork.
Upon every high mountain and lofty hill
there will be streams of running water.
On the day of the great slaughter,
when the towers fall,
The light of the moon will be like that of the sun
and the light of the sun will be seven times greater

like the light of seven days.
On the day the LORD binds up the wounds of his people,
he will heal the bruises left by his blows.

The word of the Lord.

RESPONSORIAL PSALM

Ps 147:1-2, 3-4, 5-6

R. (see Isaiah 30:18d) Blessed are all who wait for the Lord.

Praise the LORD, for he is good;
sing praise to our God, for he is gracious;
it is fitting to praise him.
The LORD rebuilds Jerusalem;
the dispersed of Israel he gathers.

R. Blessed are all who wait for the Lord.

He heals the brokenhearted
and binds up their wounds.
He tells the number of the stars;
he calls each by name.

R. Blessed are all who wait for the Lord.

Great is our LORD and mighty in power:
to his wisdom there is no limit.
The LORD sustains the lowly;
the wicked he casts to the ground.

R. Blessed are all who wait for the Lord.

ALLELUIA

Is 33:22

R. Alleluia, alleluia.
The LORD is our Judge, our Lawgiver, our King;
he it is who will save us.
R. Alleluia, alleluia.

GOSPEL

Mt 9:35–10:1, 5a, 6-8

Jesus went around to all the towns and villages,
teaching in their synagogues,
proclaiming the Gospel of the Kingdom,
and curing every disease and illness.
At the sight of the crowds, his heart was moved with pity for them
because they were troubled and abandoned,
like sheep without a shepherd.
Then he said to his disciples,
"The harvest is abundant but the laborers are few;
so ask the master of the harvest
to send out laborers for his harvest."

Then he summoned his Twelve disciples
and gave them authority over unclean spirits to drive them out
and to cure every disease and every illness.

Jesus sent out these Twelve after instructing them thus,
"Go to the lost sheep of the house of Israel.
As you go, make this proclamation: 'The Kingdom of heaven is at hand.'
Cure the sick, raise the dead,
cleanse lepers, drive out demons.
Without cost you have received; without cost you are to give."

Brothers and sisters, the Gospel of the Lord.

HOMILY:

For today's Gospel, (Matthew 9:35–10:1, 5a, 6-8,) focuses on Jesus' ministry of healing and proclamation, as well as the commissioning of His disciples, it would be apt to consider the life of St. Francis of Assisi. Known for his radical commitment to poverty and his profound connection with all of God's creation, St. Francis serves as an enduring example of someone who took Jesus' words seriously. His famous saying, "Preach the Gospel at all times; when necessary, use words," encapsulates the essence of today's Gospel message—our actions should be a living proclamation of the Gospel.

Beloved in Christ,

On this Saturday of the First Week of Advent, our Gospel offers us both a glimpse into Jesus' ministry and a model for our own Christian vocation. We see Jesus moved with compassion for the people, "because they were harassed and helpless, like sheep without a shepherd." This compassion leads to action: healing every disease and every affliction.

But Jesus doesn't stop there. He extends His mission by empowering His disciples, telling them to go forth, proclaim the kingdom, heal the sick, raise the dead, cleanse lepers, and cast out demons. In essence, they are instructed to be Christ to others, a calling that reverberates across the centuries to each one of us today.

It is a message keenly understood by saints like St. Francis of Assisi, who taught us that Gospel proclamation is not merely an oral exercise but a lived experience. In our current world, awash with social injustices, ecological crises, and spiritual malaise, there are plentiful opportunities to embody this compassion and action.

The Gospel poses a profound question for our reflection: Are we modern-day disciples who actively engage in the work of Christ? It's not enough to be sympathetic bystanders. The plight of our suffering brethren should stir us to action, just as it moved the heart of our Lord.

Christ's commission is also a call for inclusivity. He instructs His disciples to go to the "lost sheep of the house of Israel," reminding us that God's love knows no bounds. In a time where divisions often seem more prevalent than unity, this universal outlook is more important than ever. It challenges us to expand our circle of compassion and action, not limiting our love to those who look, think, or worship like us.

Let us remember the philosophers and theologians who articulated the concept of the "universal destination of goods," urging us to see the resources of the world not as personal possessions but as communal assets to be shared with those in need. In doing so, we reflect the Divine, who provides abundantly for all creation.

This Advent, let us commit ourselves anew to becoming the hands, feet, and voice of Christ in the world. As we prepare to celebrate the birth of our Savior, may we also give birth to new ways of living out His mission of love, healing, and inclusion. Amen.

PRAYER:

Almighty Father, as we gather in Your presence on this Saturday of the First Week of Advent, we are reminded by the Gospel of Matthew of the depth of Your compassion and the expansiveness of Your mission to heal and renew the world. You did not merely look upon Your people with pity; You acted, healing their illnesses and soothing their souls.

Today, we hear not only of Your works but also of Your call to us to be active participants in this divine mission. You empowered the Apostles to be carriers of Your grace, to proclaim the Kingdom, to heal, and to bring life where there was death, wholeness where there was brokenness.

We humbly ask, Lord, that You equip us, as You equipped Your Apostles, to be bearers of Your good news in today's world. Endow us with the courage to step out of our comfort zones and enter the lives of those who are suffering. Help us to be healers by our words and our deeds, ever mindful of St. Francis of Assisi's admonition to "Preach the Gospel at all times; when necessary, use words."

Holy Spirit, embolden us to reach out to the marginalized, the 'lost sheep' of today's world. Tear down the walls that divide us and guide us toward a true community grounded in love and respect for the dignity of each person.

This Advent, may our preparation for the coming of our Savior be not merely a time of personal reflection but also a season of active anticipation. May we not just prepare our homes and churches for the celebration of Christ's birth, but may we also prepare the world for His coming by living out His Gospel message of love and healing.

Through the intercession of all saints who have exemplified the essence of the Gospel, like St. Francis, may we come to live more fully in the image and likeness of Christ, the Good Shepherd.

We ask this in the name of Your Son, our Lord Jesus Christ, who lives and reigns with You and the unity of the Holy Spirit, one God, forever and ever. Amen.

MONDAY OF THE SECOND WEEK OF ADVENT

READING 1

Is 35:1-10

The desert and the parched land will exult;
the steppe will rejoice and bloom.
They will bloom with abundant flowers,
and rejoice with joyful song.
The glory of Lebanon will be given to them,
the splendor of Carmel and Sharon;
They will see the glory of the LORD,
the splendor of our God.
Strengthen the hands that are feeble,
make firm the knees that are weak,
Say to those whose hearts are frightened:
Be strong, fear not!
Here is your God,
he comes with vindication;
With divine recompense
he comes to save you.
Then will the eyes of the blind be opened,
the ears of the deaf be cleared;
Then will the lame leap like a stag,
then the tongue of the mute will sing.

Streams will burst forth in the desert,
and rivers in the steppe.
The burning sands will become pools,
and the thirsty ground, springs of water;
The abode where jackals lurk
will be a marsh for the reed and papyrus.
A highway will be there,
called the holy way;

No one unclean may pass over it,
nor fools go astray on it.
No lion will be there,
nor beast of prey go up to be met upon it.
It is for those with a journey to make,
and on it the redeemed will walk.
Those whom the LORD has ransomed will return
and enter Zion singing,
crowned with everlasting joy;
They will meet with joy and gladness,
sorrow and mourning will flee.

The word of the Lord.

RESPONSORIAL PSALM

Ps 85:9ab and 10, 11-12, 13-14

R. (Isaiah 35:4f) Our God will come to save us!

I will hear what God proclaims;
the LORD –for he proclaims peace to his people.
Near indeed is his salvation to those who fear him,
glory dwelling in our land.

R. Our God will come to save us!

Kindness and truth shall meet;
justice and peace shall kiss.
Truth shall spring out of the earth,
and justice shall look down from heaven.

R. Our God will come to save us!
The LORD himself will give his benefits;
our land shall yield its increase.
Justice shall walk before him,
and salvation, along the way of his steps.

R. Our God will come to save us!

ALLELUIA

R. Alleluia, alleluia.
Behold the king will come, the Lord of the earth,
and he himself will lift the yoke of our captivity.
R. Alleluia, alleluia.

GOSPEL

Lk 5:17-26

One day as Jesus was teaching,
Pharisees and teachers of the law,
who had come from every village of Galilee and Judea and Jerusalem,
were sitting there,
and the power of the Lord was with him for healing.
And some men brought on a stretcher a man who was paralyzed;
they were trying to bring him in and set him in his presence.
But not finding a way to bring him in because of the crowd,
they went up on the roof
and lowered him on the stretcher through the tiles
into the middle in front of Jesus.
When Jesus saw their faith, he said,
"As for you, your sins are forgiven."

Then the scribes and Pharisees began to ask themselves,
"Who is this who speaks blasphemies?
Who but God alone can forgive sins?"
Jesus knew their thoughts and said to them in reply,
"What are you thinking in your hearts?
Which is easier, to say, 'Your sins are forgiven,'
or to say, 'Rise and walk'?
But that you may know
that the Son of Man has authority on earth to forgive sins"–
he said to the one who was paralyzed,
"I say to you, rise, pick up your stretcher, and go home."

He stood up immediately before them,
picked up what he had been lying on,
and went home, glorifying God.
Then astonishment seized them all and they glorified God,

and, struck with awe, they said,
"We have seen incredible things today."

Brothers and sisters, the Gospel of the Lord.

HOMILY:

Consider the life of St. Augustine, a man who lived in moral paralysis for years, entangled in worldly pleasures and intellectual pride. It took a direct confrontation with God's Word—reading from the Book of Romans—to shake him from his stupor. His friends and mother, St. Monica, must have felt as though they were carrying a paralytic to Jesus for years through their prayers and supplications. When Augustine finally experienced his conversion, the "roof" of his pride was removed, and he was lowered into the healing presence of Christ. This transformative moment echoes the Gospel story we contemplate today—how faith, community, and the touch of Christ can heal our deepest ailments.

Dearest brothers and sisters in Christ,

As we enter this Monday of the Second Week of Advent, we are greeted by the Gospel of Luke, which recounts the story of a paralyzed man healed by Jesus. This tale unfolds not just as a physical healing but as a multi-dimensional miracle, encompassing the man's physical, spiritual, and communal life.

Observe, firstly, that the paralyzed man was not alone; he was brought to Jesus by his friends. They display a determined love, going so far as to lower him through the roof to reach Christ. This act highlights the value and efficacy of communal faith. As Christians, we are called to lift one another up, to carry those in our community closer to Jesus, just as St. Monica's relentless prayers and Christian example helped guide her son Augustine toward God.

Secondly, Jesus does not merely heal the man's physical paralysis; He first addresses the paralysis of sin by forgiving him. It is a vivid reminder that spiritual healing often precedes or accompanies physical or emotional healing. This Advent, we too should seek the forgiveness that comes only from reconciliation with God, a reconciliation made possible by the birth, life, death, and resurrection of Jesus Christ.

Lastly, it is worth noting that Jesus performs this miracle under the scrutinizing gaze of the Pharisees and teachers of the Law. His actions serve as a testament to His divinity and authority. But they also serve as a critique of an approach to religion that is legalistic, detached, and judgmental. We must be vigilant to ensure that our faith does not become an empty shell of rituals and laws, but remains a vibrant relationship with the living God, marked by active love for our neighbors.

Taking inspiration from philosophers who emphasize the importance of authentic existence, let us endeavor to lead lives that are fully engaged, not paralyzed by sin, indifference, or intellectual pride. Like St. Augustine, may we allow God to break through the "roofs" that confine us, so that we can be fully restored—mind, body, and soul—in His healing presence.

Let us use this season of Advent to break down the barriers—whether they be of sin, of complacency, or of isolation—that prevent us from drawing near to Christ and experiencing His transformative love. Amen.

PRAYER:

Gracious and Merciful God,
On this Monday of the Second Week of Advent, we are confronted with the miraculous account from the Gospel of Luke of the healing of the paralyzed man. This man, burdened by his physical ailment, was brought into Your presence by friends filled with faith. Today, we bring before You our own burdens—physical, emotional, and spiritual—seeking Your healing touch.

Lord, we are reminded that before You addressed the man's physical condition, You offered him something even more significant: the forgiveness of his sins. During this season of Advent, grant us the grace to seek reconciliation with You and with one another. Like St. Augustine, who was brought to a profound transformation through Your Word and the prayers of his community, may we too experience conversion of heart.

We pray also for the grace of community and fellowship, following the example of the friends who brought the paralyzed man to You. Empower us to bear one another's burdens and to bring each other closer to You in faith. Let us be the hands and feet that carry those in need, the hearts that believe even when circumstances seem impossible, and the spirits that pray continuously for the welfare of all.

May the Pharisees and teachers of the Law in today's Gospel prompt us to examine our own approach to religion. Keep us from the rigidity that focuses solely on law and neglects the weightier matters of justice, mercy, and faith. Reinvigorate our practice of faith, filling it with love, humility, and a yearning for Your kingdom.

O God, as we anticipate the coming of Your Son, our Lord Jesus Christ, let this Advent season be a time of renewal for us. May it be an occasion for both personal and communal transformation, so that when we celebrate the birth of our Savior, we may do so as a people more fully alive in Your love and grace.

Through the intercession of all the saints who have walked the path of righteousness, especially those like St. Augustine who found

*healing and conversion in You, guide us to a more profound faith
and a more vibrant community.*

*We ask all this in the name of Jesus Christ, our Lord and Savior,
who lives and reigns with You and the unity of the Holy Spirit,
one God, forever and ever. Amen.*

TUESDAY OF THE SECOND WEEK OF ADVENT

READING 1

Is 40:1-11

Comfort, give comfort to my people,
says your God.
Speak tenderly to Jerusalem, and proclaim to her
that her service is at an end,
her guilt is expiated;
Indeed, she has received from the hand of the LORD
double for all her sins.

A voice cries out:
In the desert prepare the way of the LORD!
Make straight in the wasteland a highway for our God!
Every valley shall be filled in,
every mountain and hill shall be made low;
The rugged land shall be made a plain,
the rough country, a broad valley.
Then the glory of the LORD shall be revealed,
and all people shall see it together;
for the mouth of the LORD has spoken.

A voice says, "Cry out!"
I answer, "What shall I cry out?"
"All flesh is grass,
and all their glory like the flower of the field.
The grass withers, the flower wilts,
when the breath of the LORD blows upon it.
So then, the people is the grass.
Though the grass withers and the flower wilts,
the word of our God stands forever."
Go up onto a high mountain,

Zion, herald of glad tidings;
Cry out at the top of your voice,
Jerusalem, herald of good news!
Fear not to cry out
and say to the cities of Judah:
Here is your God!
Here comes with power
the Lord GOD,
who rules by his strong arm;
Here is his reward with him,
his recompense before him.
Like a shepherd he feeds his flock;
in his arms he gathers the lambs,
Carrying them in his bosom,
and leading the ewes with care.

The word of the Lord.

RESPONSORIAL PSALM

Ps 96:1-2, 3 and 10ac, 11-12, 13

R. (see Isaiah 40:10ab) The Lord our God comes with power.

Sing to the LORD a new song;
sing to the LORD, all you lands.
Sing to the LORD; bless his name;
announce his salvation, day after day.

R. The Lord our God comes with power.

Tell his glory among the nations;
among all peoples, his wondrous deeds.
Say among the nations: The LORD is king;
he governs the peoples with equity.

R. The Lord our God comes with power.

Let the heavens be glad and the earth rejoice;
let the sea and what fills it resound;
let the plains be joyful and all that is in them!
Then let all the trees of the forest rejoice.

R. The Lord our God comes with power.

They shall exult before the LORD, for he comes;
for he comes to rule the earth.
He shall rule the world with justice
and the peoples with his constancy.

R. The Lord our God comes with power.

ALLELUIA

R. Alleluia, alleluia.
The day of the Lord is near;
Behold, he comes to save us.
R. Alleluia, alleluia.

GOSPEL

Mt 18:12-14

Jesus said to his disciples:
"What is your opinion?
If a man has a hundred sheep and one of them goes astray,
will he not leave the ninety-nine in the hills
and go in search of the stray?
And if he finds it, amen, I say to you, he rejoices more over it
than over the ninety-nine that did not stray.
In just the same way, it is not the will of your heavenly Father
that one of these little ones be lost."

Brothers and sisters, the Gospel of the Lord.

HOMILY:

The story of the renowned philosopher Søren Kierkegaard comes to mind when contemplating today's Gospel. Kierkegaard told a story about a king who, despite his power and wealth, fell in love with a humble maiden from a distant village. The king faced a dilemma: He could arrive in grandeur to ask for her hand, but would she love him for himself or for his power? In the end, the king chose to shed his royal robes and meet her dressed as a commoner, sacrificing his dignity for a chance at genuine love. In this act of "kenosis" or self-emptying, he risked losing all to gain everything. This mirrors the way our Heavenly King risks the "ninety-nine" to go after the lost one.

Beloved in Christ,

As we gather in prayer and contemplation on this Tuesday of the Second Week of Advent, we are invited to meditate upon the Gospel of Matthew. In today's reading, we encounter the Good Shepherd, who leaves the ninety-nine sheep in the hills to go in search of the one that has gone astray.

This parable encapsulates the very essence of Divine Love—a love that is willing to sacrifice for the good of the other. Just as Søren Kierkegaard's king risked his stature and comfort to seek authentic love, so does God empty Himself, taking on human form in Jesus Christ, to bring back the lost, the wayward, and the broken.

The story calls us to consider: Are we among the ninety-nine, safe and content within the fold, or are we the one, lost and seeking a way back to God? The reality is, at different moments in our lives, we are both. Sometimes we are secure in our faith, and at other times we are in dire need of spiritual recuperation. Just like St. Augustine, whose life vacillated between spiritual dryness and divine intimacy, we are on a journey back to the Shepherd, who never ceases to search for us.

This Advent season offers us a renewed opportunity for introspection, to think deeply about our spiritual state. Are we complacent, assuming we are among the ninety-nine, or are we actively participating in our own salvation and the salvation of others? We are called to join Christ in His mission, to help bring back the lost sheep among us—those estranged from family, community, and God Himself.

Moreover, it serves as a reminder not to sit in judgment like the Pharisees, who often looked down on those who were lost. Remember, in God's eyes, each one of us is that precious "one" worth going after, worth sacrificing everything for.

So, let us prepare ourselves this Advent, not just with the external trappings of the season but with a deep interior renewal. Like St. Francis of Assisi, who saw God in all of creation and dedicated himself to a life of poverty and service, may we embody the qualities of the Good Shepherd. Let us reach out to the lost, the forgotten, and the downtrodden, for by doing so, we serve Christ Himself.

May this season be a journey back to the heart of God, our Good Shepherd, who assures us that it is "not the will of your heavenly Father that one of these little ones be lost." Amen.

PRAYER:

Almighty and Loving God,
As we gather in this season of Advent, we come before You with hearts yearning for Your guidance and Your peace. Today, we contemplate the Gospel of Matthew, where Jesus, our Good Shepherd, seeks out the lost sheep, leaving the ninety-nine in the hills to retrieve the one who has strayed.

Lord, we humbly ask for the grace to be ever conscious of Your ceaseless search for each one of us, particularly when we wander away from Your loving embrace. Just as St. Monica never ceased praying for her wayward son, Augustine, may we also be persistent in our prayers for those who are spiritually lost. Grant us the fervor to pray and act in such a way that brings others closer to You.

In our own moments of wandering, feeling distant from Your grace, remind us that You are the Shepherd who knows no bounds in seeking the welfare of Your flock. May we have the courage to heed Your voice and return to the path of righteousness and peace.

Lord, give us the compassion to be shepherds in our own right, echoing Your boundless love for all. Encourage us to step out of our comfort zones, to seek out those who are estranged and lonely, those who need a healing touch, a kind word, or a gesture of love. May we be Your hands and feet in a world desperate for Your grace.

Through the example of saints like Francis of Assisi, who embraced the marginalized and exemplified the self-sacrificing love of the Good Shepherd, help us to be instruments of Your peace and heralds of Your kingdom.

O Divine Shepherd, guide us in the ways of wisdom and understanding, that we may prepare adequately for the coming of our Savior, Jesus Christ. It is His promise of redemption that we await this Advent season—a promise that assures us that not one of us is beyond the reach of Your saving love.

We offer this prayer in the name of Your Son, our Lord Jesus Christ, who lives and reigns with You and the Holy Spirit, one God, forever and ever. Amen

WEDNESDAY OF THE SECOND WEEK OF ADVENT

READING 1

Is 40:25-31

To whom can you liken me as an equal?
says the Holy One.
Lift up your eyes on high
and see who has created these things:
He leads out their army and numbers them,
calling them all by name.
By his great might and the strength of his power
not one of them is missing!
Why, O Jacob, do you say,
and declare, O Israel,
"My way is hidden from the LORD,
and my right is disregarded by my God"?

Do you not know
or have you not heard?
The LORD is the eternal God,
creator of the ends of the earth.
He does not faint nor grow weary,
and his knowledge is beyond scrutiny.
He gives strength to the fainting;
for the weak he makes vigor abound.
Though young men faint and grow weary,
and youths stagger and fall,
They that hope in the LORD will renew their strength,
they will soar as with eagles' wings;
They will run and not grow weary,
walk and not grow faint.

The word of the Lord.

RESPONSORIAL PSALM

Ps 103:1-2, 3-4, 8 and 10

R. (1) O bless the Lord, my soul!

Bless the LORD, O my soul;
and all my being, bless his holy name.
Bless the LORD, O my soul,
and forget not all his benefits.

R. O bless the Lord, my soul!

He pardons all your iniquities,
he heals all your ills.
He redeems your life from destruction,
he crowns you with kindness and compassion.

R. O bless the Lord, my soul!

Merciful and gracious is the LORD,
slow to anger and abounding in kindness.
Not according to our sins does he deal with us,
nor does he requite us according to our crimes.

R. O bless the Lord, my soul!

ALLELUIA

R. Alleluia, alleluia.
Behold, the Lord comes to save his people;
blessed are those prepared to meet him.
R. Alleluia, alleluia.

GOSPEL

Mt 11:28-30

Jesus said to the crowds:
"Come to me, all you who labor and are burdened,
and I will give you rest.
Take my yoke upon you and learn from me,
for I am meek and humble of heart;
and you will find rest for yourselves.
For my yoke is easy, and my burden light."

Brothers and sisters, the Gospel of the Lord.

HOMILY:

There's an age-old tale about an elderly man who used to visit the ocean to do his writing. He had a habit of walking on the beach every morning before he began his work. One day, as he was walking along the shore, he saw a young man reaching down to the sand, picking up something, and gently throwing it back into the ocean.

Approaching the young man, he asked, "What are you doing?" The young man replied, "Throwing starfish back into the ocean. The surf is up and the tide is going out. If I don't throw them back, they'll die." The old man laughed and said, "Do you realize there are miles and miles of beach and hundreds of starfish? You can't possibly make a difference!"

After listening politely, the young man bent down, picked up another starfish, and threw it into the surf. Then, smiling at the man, he said, "I made a difference for that one."

Dear Brothers and Sisters in Christ,

As we proceed in this blessed Advent season, we encounter Christ's words in the Gospel of Matthew: "Come to me, all you who labor and are burdened, and I will give you rest."

These words remind us that we are all carrying burdens—perhaps of sin, despair, or even the complexities and stresses of daily life. In the eyes of God, however, no burden is too heavy that it can't be shared with Him. Much like the young man in the story who believed that even one act could make a difference, Jesus invites us to bring even our smallest cares to Him, for in His divine wisdom and mercy, no concern is insignificant.

St. Augustine famously said, "Thou hast made us for Thyself, O Lord, and our heart is restless until it finds its rest in Thee." We are all restless starfish, so to speak, yearning for the eternal ocean of God's love. And the Lord, like the diligent young man, picks us up one by one and guides us toward that eternal rest.

During Advent, we are called to not only receive Christ's comfort but also to be bearers of this comfort to others. It's easy to be overwhelmed by the vastness of suffering in the world, thinking our efforts inconsequential. But remember, even if we make a difference to just 'one starfish,' our actions have infinite worth in the eyes of God.

St. Teresa of Calcutta once said, "We can do no great things, only small things with great love." As we await the coming of our Savior, let us bring to Him all our labors and burdens, trusting in His restorative love. And may we also strive to be sources of comfort and rest to those who labor and are burdened around us.

It is through such small acts of love that we prepare the way of the Lord, making the paths straight for His triumphant coming. Let us, therefore, come to Him, for His yoke is easy, and His burden is light. Amen.

PRAYER:

Most Gracious Heavenly Father,

On this Wednesday of the Second Week of Advent, we come before You with the Gospel of Matthew deep in our hearts: "Come to me, all you who labor and are burdened, and I will give you rest."

Lord, these words are like a soothing balm for our weary souls. You know the weights that we carry—the anxieties, the uncertainties, the sorrows, and the sins. We lay them before Your altar now, asking for the peace and rest that only You can provide.

Just as St. John of the Cross found solace in You during his dark night of the soul, so too do we seek Your divine comfort. Fill us with the Holy Spirit, so that we may find the strength to face our daily challenges, no matter how daunting they seem. Inspire us to take on Your yoke, which is easy, and Your burden, which is light.

As we prepare for the coming of Your Son, Jesus Christ, make our hearts a fitting cradle for Him—a place where He may lay His head and find a home. Help us to heed the wisdom of St. Augustine, who reminds us that our hearts will remain restless until they find their ultimate rest in You.

Almighty God, we pray that this Advent may be a time of spiritual rejuvenation for us. Like the expectant Virgin Mary, may we too say 'yes' to Your divine will, and trust in Your impeccable timing. Let the peace that surpasses all understanding settle over us, as we wait in joyful hope for the birth of our Savior, who promises to lift our burdens and give us rest.

We offer this prayer in the name of Your Son, our Lord Jesus Christ, who lives and reigns with You and the unity of the Holy Spirit, one God, forever and ever. Amen.

THURSDAY OF THE SECOND WEEK OF ADVENT

READING 1

Is 41:13-20

I am the LORD, your God,
who grasp your right hand;
It is I who say to you, "Fear not,
I will help you."
Fear not, O worm Jacob,
O maggot Israel;
I will help you, says the LORD;
your redeemer is the Holy One of Israel.
I will make of you a threshing sledge,
sharp, new, and double-edged,
To thresh the mountains and crush them,
to make the hills like chaff.
When you winnow them, the wind shall carry them off
and the storm shall scatter them.
But you shall rejoice in the LORD,
and glory in the Holy One of Israel.

The afflicted and the needy seek water in vain,
their tongues are parched with thirst.
I, the LORD, will answer them;
I, the God of Israel, will not forsake them.
I will open up rivers on the bare heights,
and fountains in the broad valleys;
I will turn the desert into a marshland,
and the dry ground into springs of water.
I will plant in the desert the cedar,
acacia, myrtle, and olive;
I will set in the wasteland the cypress,
together with the plane tree and the pine,

That all may see and know,
observe and understand,
That the hand of the LORD has done this,
the Holy One of Israel has created it.

The word of the Lord.

RESPONSORIAL PSALM

Ps 145:1 and 9, 10-11, 12-13ab

R. (8) The Lord is gracious and merciful; slow to anger, and of great kindness.

I will extol you, O my God and King,
and I will bless your name forever and ever.
The LORD is good to all
and compassionate toward all his works.

R. The Lord is gracious and merciful; slow to anger, and of great kindness.

Let all your works give you thanks, O LORD,
and let your faithful ones bless you.
Let them discourse of the glory of your Kingdom
and speak of your might.

R. The Lord is gracious and merciful; slow to anger, and of great kindness.

Let them make known to men your might
and the glorious splendor of your Kingdom.
Your Kingdom is a Kingdom for all ages,
and your dominion endures through all generations.

R. The Lord is gracious and merciful; slow to anger, and of great kindness.

ALLELUIA

See Is 45:8

R. Alleluia, alleluia.
Let the clouds rain down the Just One,
and the earth bring forth a Savior.
R. Alleluia, alleluia.

GOSPEL

Mt 11:11-15

Jesus said to the crowds:
"Amen, I say to you,
among those born of women
there has been none greater than John the Baptist;
yet the least in the Kingdom of heaven is greater than he.
From the days of John the Baptist until now,
the Kingdom of heaven suffers violence,
and the violent are taking it by force.
All the prophets and the law prophesied up to the time of John.
And if you are willing to accept it,
he is Elijah, the one who is to come.
Whoever has ears ought to hear."

Brothers and sisters, the Gospel of the Lord.

HOMILY:

In the medieval period, a certain king wanted to build a cathedral as a testament to his faith. He employed various artisans, builders, and craftsmen for the massive undertaking. One day, as he visited the construction site, he interacted with three masons who were chipping stones. Curious, the king asked each one, "What are you doing?"

The first mason responded, "I'm chipping stones, Your Majesty, as you can plainly see." The second mason replied, "I'm building a wall, sire." However, the third mason looked up, his eyes shining with inspiration, and declared, "I'm building a cathedral, Your Majesty, a home for God."

Dearly Beloved,

As we journey through the season of Advent, today's Gospel from Matthew presents us with the enigmatic figure of John the Baptist. Jesus, in His profound wisdom, asserts, "Amen, I say to you, among those born of women there has been none greater than John the Baptist; yet the least in the kingdom of heaven is greater than he."

Much like the third mason in our story who saw beyond his immediate task to the grand vision of building a cathedral, John the Baptist had an acute awareness of his purpose. He was not merely 'chipping stones' or 'building walls'; he was preparing the way for the Kingdom of Heaven. Though cloaked in rough garments and situated in the wilderness, his vision was not confined to his immediate surroundings or role. He knew he was part of a grand divine design, a precursor to the Messiah.

The greatness of John, according to Jesus, does not lie in his austerity or his courage to speak the truth. Rather, it lies in his deep understanding of his role in God's salvific plan—a role he accepted humbly, acknowledging that he was unworthy to even untie the sandals of the coming Messiah. St. Augustine reminds us that humility is the foundation of all virtues, and John the Baptist exemplifies this through his life and mission.

However, the Gospel paradoxically states that "the least in the Kingdom of Heaven is greater than he." This phrase invites us to realize that as members of the Church, recipients of the sacraments, and followers of a risen Christ, we are beneficiaries of a grace that even John could only foresee. The least in the kingdom are those who live in the humility of John but are privileged to know the fullness of God's revelation in Christ Jesus.

In this Advent season, let us strive to be like the third mason and John the Baptist—mindful of the grandeur of God's overarching plan for humanity. Let us not just 'chip stones' but actively participate in building the Kingdom of Heaven here on earth.

Like St. Francis of Assisi, may we be instruments of God's peace and love, and in doing so, prepare a worthy abode for our coming King. Amen.

PRAYER:

Almighty and Everlasting God,

On this Thursday of the Second Week of Advent, we are reminded by Your Word of the unique role John the Baptist played in preparing the way for Your beloved Son, our Lord Jesus Christ. With humility and conviction, John proclaimed a message of repentance and heralded the coming of the Kingdom of Heaven.

Inspired by today's Gospel from Matthew, we offer our prayers to You, acknowledging our own need for humility, conversion, and readiness for Your coming Kingdom. Help us to appreciate the depth and richness of Your divine plan for us and the world, so that we may not be mere 'chippers of stone,' but active participants in building Your Kingdom on Earth.

Grant us the grace to be like John the Baptist, unwavering in our faith and resolute in our mission. We recall the words of St. Therese of Lisieux, who said, "My vocation is love." May our vocation be one of love and service, humble yet confident in its divine purpose.

We also pray for those who have not yet heard Your message or who have turned away from it. May they, too, find the transformative power of Your love and the boundless joy of Your eternal promise.

As we continue our Advent journey, we keep in mind that the 'least in the Kingdom of Heaven is greater than John the Baptist.' This profound truth fills us with awe and responsibility, reminding us that our role in Your plan is both a gift and a calling. May we live up to this high calling, embracing it fully with a heart enriched by humility, faith, and love.

We offer this prayer through Your Son, Jesus Christ, who came to show us the way to eternal life, and who lives and reigns with You in the unity of the Holy Spirit, one God, forever and ever. Amen.

FRIDAY OF THE SECOND WEEK OF ADVENT

READING 1

Is 48:17-19

Thus says the LORD, your redeemer,
the Holy One of Israel:
I, the LORD, your God,
teach you what is for your good,
and lead you on the way you should go.
If you would hearken to my commandments,
your prosperity would be like a river,
and your vindication like the waves of the sea;
Your descendants would be like the sand,
and those born of your stock like its grains,
Their name never cut off
or blotted out from my presence.

The word of the Lord.

RESPONSORIAL PSALM

Ps 1:1-2, 3, 4 and 6

R. (see John 8:12) Those who follow you, Lord, will have the light of life.

Blessed the man who follows not
the counsel of the wicked
Nor walks in the way of sinners,
nor sits in the company of the insolent,
But delights in the law of the LORD
and meditates on his law day and night.
R. Those who follow you, Lord, will have the light of life.

He is like a tree
planted near running water,
That yields its fruit in due season,
and whose leaves never fade.
Whatever he does, prospers.

R. Those who follow you, Lord, will have the light of life.

Not so the wicked, not so;
they are like chaff which the wind drives away.
For the LORD watches over the way of the just,
but the way of the wicked vanishes.

R. Those who follow you, Lord, will have the light of life.

ALLELUIA

R. Alleluia, alleluia.
The Lord will come; go out to meet him!
He is the prince of peace.
R. Alleluia, alleluia.

GOSPEL

Mt 11:16-19

Jesus said to the crowds:
"To what shall I compare this generation?
It is like children who sit in marketplaces and call to one another,
'We played the flute for you, but you did not dance,
we sang a dirge but you did not mourn.'
For John came neither eating nor drinking, and they said,
'He is possessed by a demon.'
The Son of Man came eating and drinking and they said,
'Look, he is a glutton and a drunkard,
a friend of tax collectors and sinners.'
But wisdom is vindicated by her works."

Brothers and sisters, the Gospel of the Lord.

HOMILY:

In a small village, there were two brothers who lived next door to each other. One was a pious man who attended church regularly, while the other was a skeptic who never set foot inside a sanctuary. However, every Sunday after returning from Mass, the religious brother would find his skeptical sibling doing acts of kindness—helping a neighbor fix a roof, feeding stray animals, or planting trees. When questioned about his refusal to attend church, the skeptical brother would always say, "I find my own way to worship."

Dearest in Christ,

The Gospel of Matthew for this day offers us a very intriguing and, might I say, challenging message. Jesus draws a comparison between His generation and children who cannot be pleased, no matter what is offered to them. "We played the flute for you, but you did not dance; we sang a dirge, but you did not mourn." It speaks to the human tendency to be critical and resistant, to find fault rather than find faith.

In today's Gospel, Jesus is reminding us of the futility of a judgmental attitude. He gives the examples of John the Baptist and Himself, who, despite their vastly different approaches to ministry—John in austere penitence and Jesus in compassionate engagement—both faced criticism and disbelief. It's like the story of the two brothers, one finding God in the Church, and the other finding God in acts of love. And yet, they failed to recognize the value in each other's forms of worship. Isn't it often the case in our lives that we become too rigid in our own paradigms that we fail to recognize God's manifold and diverse presence?

St. Thomas Aquinas, one of the great theological luminaries of the Church, stated that "To one who has faith, no explanation is necessary. To one without faith, no explanation is possible." John the Baptist came neither eating nor drinking, and he was criticized. Jesus came eating and drinking, and He too was criticized. The problem was not with John or Jesus but with the people whose hearts were hardened, who had formed judgments without seeking understanding.

As we progress through this Advent season, let us keep an open heart, one that is willing to find God not just in our personal preferences but in the diverse manifestations of grace and holiness around us. Advent is a time of expectant waiting, and how can we wait expectantly if our hearts are closed?

We are called to dance to the music of God's grace and to mourn the sins that separate us from His love. In the words of St. Augustine, "God loves each of us as if there were only one of us." May we, too, learn to love God and each other, free from judgment and open to the manifold ways He speaks to us.

May this message guide us as we prepare for the celebration of the Nativity of our Lord, the moment when Heaven touched Earth, reminding us that God can be found in the most unexpected places, if only we open our hearts to see. Amen.

PRAYER:

Heavenly Father,

On this Friday of the Second Week of Advent, we are reminded by the Gospel according to Matthew that Your divine wisdom manifests in various ways, often beyond human understanding. Your Son, our Lord Jesus Christ, and John the Baptist encountered criticism and misunderstanding despite their different styles of proclaiming Your Kingdom. How often do we too, Lord, become judges of Your diverse manifestations of grace?

In the quiet of our hearts, we seek Your wisdom. We desire a wisdom that does not sit in judgment but embraces with love, a wisdom that does not divide but unifies, a wisdom that sees You in the multitude of ways You make Yourself known to us. As the Church Father St. John Chrysostom said, "Nothing is more fallacious than wealth. It is a hostile comrade, a domestic enemy." Let us not be trapped by the wealth of our prejudices and judgments, but be enriched by the wisdom that comes from You.

We pray, Lord, that You endow us with the spiritual discernment to recognize You not only in what is familiar and comforting but also in what challenges us and takes us out of our comfort zones. Let our hearts dance to the music of Your grace and let our souls mourn for the ways we have turned away from You.

In this season of Advent, a time of preparation and expectation, guide our steps toward the manger and our souls toward salvation. Let us be like the children who are content in both mourning and dancing because they trust in the goodness of their Father. Illuminate our hearts with the advent candles of hope, peace, joy, and love, that we may be light unto others, leading them to the eternal light that is Christ Jesus.

We offer this prayer through the same Christ, our Lord, who lives and reigns with You and the unity of the Holy Spirit reigns as one God, forever and ever. Amen.

SATURDAY OF THE SECOND WEEK OF ADVENT

READING 1

Sir 48:1-4, 9-11

In those days,
like a fire there appeared the prophet Elijah
whose words were as a flaming furnace.
Their staff of bread he shattered,
in his zeal he reduced them to straits;
By the Lord's word he shut up the heavens
and three times brought down fire.
How awesome are you, Elijah, in your wondrous deeds!
Whose glory is equal to yours?
You were taken aloft in a whirlwind of fire,
in a chariot with fiery horses.
You were destined, it is written, in time to come
to put an end to wrath before the day of the LORD,
To turn back the hearts of fathers toward their sons,
and to re-establish the tribes of Jacob.
Blessed is he who shall have seen you
and who falls asleep in your friendship.

The word of the Lord.

RESPONSORIAL PSALM

Ps 80:2ac and 3b, 15-16, 18-19

R. (4) Lord, make us turn to you; let us see your face and we shall be saved.

O shepherd of Israel, hearken,
From your throne upon the cherubim, shine forth.
Rouse your power.

R. Lord, make us turn to you; let us see your face and we shall be saved.

Once again, O LORD of hosts,
look down from heaven, and see;
Take care of this vine,
and protect what your right hand has planted
the son of man whom you yourself made strong.

R. Lord, make us turn to you; let us see your face and we shall be saved.

May your help be with the man of your right hand,
with the son of man whom you yourself made strong.
Then we will no more withdraw from you;
give us new life, and we will call upon your name.

R. Lord, make us turn to you; let us see your face and we shall be saved.

ALLELUIA

Lk 3:4, 6

R. Alleluia, alleluia.
Prepare the way of the Lord, make straight his paths:
All flesh shall see the salvation of God.
R. Alleluia, alleluia.

GOSPEL

Mt 17:9a, 10-13

As they were coming down from the mountain,
the disciples asked Jesus,
"Why do the scribes say that Elijah must come first?"
He said in reply, "Elijah will indeed come and restore all things;
but I tell you that Elijah has already come,
and they did not recognize him but did to him whatever they pleased.
So also will the Son of Man suffer at their hands."
Then the disciples understood
that he was speaking to them of John the Baptist.

Brothers and sisters, the Gospel of the Lord.

HOMILY:

There was once a lighthouse keeper who had served faithfully for many years. He had weathered countless storms and guided numerous vessels safely to shore. In his old age, he was informed that his lighthouse was to be automated and that his services were no longer required. Disheartened, he left his post but often returned to the lighthouse, standing silently, watching the automated light do its work. When asked why he returned, he replied, "The light may still shine, but it cannot hear the ships' horns in the fog or sound the foghorn to guide them safely. It's not just about giving light; it's also about listening and responding."

Dear brothers and sisters in Christ,

As we gather on this Saturday of the Second Week of Advent, we are presented with the Gospel of Matthew which recounts the disciples' confusion about the role of Elijah, who was prophesied to return before the coming of the Messiah. Jesus reveals to them that Elijah has indeed come, in the person of John the Baptist. However, like the light without the lighthouse keeper, the people failed to recognize John's role; they did not listen or respond appropriately.

It serves us a poignant reminder that God's messages and messengers are not always met with the reception they deserve. As with John the Baptist, who lived a life of stern penitence and prophetic vigor, so too are many of God's messengers misunderstood, mistreated, or ignored. Saint Athanasius, a Church Father and defender of Christian orthodoxy, once said, "God became man so that man might become god." The Incarnation was the ultimate message, and yet, how often do we fail to recognize its implications in our daily lives?

The wisdom of our faith teaches us to see beyond the literal, to recognize the spirit of Elijah in John the Baptist, and by extension, to recognize the workings of God in unexpected places and faces. The lighthouse may be automated, but it cannot listen to the cries of struggling ships. We are called to be more than just receivers of light; we are called to be responsive, to hear the horns in the fog and to sound the foghorns, guiding others toward God's grace.

As we continue our journey in Advent, preparing for the commemoration of Christ's Nativity and in joyful hope of His Second Coming, let us be mindful of the role each of us plays in God's plan. We are not merely bystanders or passive recipients of grace; we are active participants, called to both recognize and proclaim God's merciful love.

Let us pray that we may be like John the Baptist, carrying the spirit of Elijah, preparing the way for the Lord in the hearts of those we meet, ever attentive to God's call and ever responsive to His divine promptings.

May the Lord bless us and guide us as we continue to prepare our hearts for the coming of our Savior, Jesus Christ. Amen.

PRAYER:

Almighty and Everlasting God,

As we reflect on today's Gospel, where the prophetic role of John the Baptist is clarified to the disciples, we are reminded of Your marvelous plan unfolding throughout history. Your ways are not our ways, and Your thoughts are not our thoughts. We ask that You bestow upon us the gift of discernment, that we might recognize the "Elijahs" of our own time—those who prepare the way for a deeper understanding and experience of You.

St. Augustine once said, "Faith is to believe what you do not see; the reward of this faith is to see what you believe." We have not seen Elijah or John the Baptist, nor have we witnessed their sacrifices first-hand, but we believe in their divine missions. May our faith be rewarded by seeing the evidence of Your work in our lives and in the world around us.

Lord, during this blessed season of Advent, grant us the wisdom to recognize the signs of Your presence among us. Let us not be like those who did not understand the role of John the Baptist, turning away from the voice crying out in the wilderness. Instead, equip us to be modern-day heralds of Your Word, preparing the way for the Lord in the lives of those we encounter.

Just as the disciples were instructed not to tell anyone about the vision until the Son of Man had risen from the dead, so let us be prudent in our own proclamations, guided by Your Spirit, timing, and wisdom. May we be instruments that reflect Your light, not blinding or confusing, but guiding and illuminating the path to You.

We entrust this prayer to Your loving care, confident in Your plan and timing for all things. May Your will be done on earth as it is in heaven, as we continue to watch and wait for the glorious coming of our Savior, Jesus Christ. Amen.

MONDAY OF THE THIRD WEEK OF ADVENT

READING 1

Nm 24:2-7, 15-17a

When Balaam raised his eyes and saw Israel encamped, tribe by tribe,
the spirit of God came upon him,
and he gave voice to his oracle:

The utterance of Balaam, son of Beor,
the utterance of a man whose eye is true,
The utterance of one who hears what God says,
and knows what the Most High knows,
Of one who sees what the Almighty sees,
enraptured, and with eyes unveiled:
How goodly are your tents, O Jacob;
your encampments, O Israel!
They are like gardens beside a stream,
like the cedars planted by the LORD.
His wells shall yield free-flowing waters,
he shall have the sea within reach;
His king shall rise higher,
and his royalty shall be exalted.

Then Balaam gave voice to his oracle:

The utterance of Balaam, son of Beor,
the utterance of the man whose eye is true,
The utterance of one who hears what God says,
and knows what the Most High knows,
Of one who sees what the Almighty sees,
enraptured, and with eyes unveiled.
I see him, though not now;
I behold him, though not near:

A star shall advance from Jacob,
and a staff shall rise from Israel.

The word of the Lord.

RESPONSORIAL PSALM

Ps 25:4-5ab, 6 and 7bc, 8-9

R.(4) Teach me your ways, O Lord.

Your ways, O LORD, make known to me;
teach me your paths,
Guide me in your truth and teach me,
for you are God my savior.

R. Teach me your ways, O Lord.

Remember that your compassion, O LORD,
and your kindness are from of old.
In your kindness remember me,
because of your goodness, O LORD.

R. Teach me your ways, O Lord.

Good and upright is the LORD;
thus he shows sinners the way.
He guides the humble to justice,
he teaches the humble his way.

R. Teach me your ways, O Lord.

ALLELUIA

Ps 85:8

R. Alleluia, alleluia.
Show us, LORD, your love,
and grant us your salvation.
R. Alleluia, alleluia.

GOSPEL

Mt 21:23-27

When Jesus had come into the temple area,
the chief priests and the elders of the people approached him
as he was teaching and said,
"By what authority are you doing these things?
And who gave you this authority?"
Jesus said to them in reply,
"I shall ask you one question, and if you answer it for me,
then I shall tell you by what authority I do these things.
Where was John's baptism from?
Was it of heavenly or of human origin?"
They discussed this among themselves and said,
"If we say 'Of heavenly origin,' he will say to us,
'Then why did you not believe him?'
But if we say, 'Of human origin,' we fear the crowd,
for they all regard John as a prophet."
So they said to Jesus in reply, "We do not know."
He himself said to them,
"Neither shall I tell you by what authority I do these things."

Brothers and sisters, the Gospel of the Lord.

HOMILY:

A renowned philosopher once stood before his class with a large jar. He filled it with rocks and asked if it was full. The class agreed that it was. He then poured pebbles into the jar, filling the spaces between the rocks. Again, he asked if it was full, and they concurred. Finally, he poured sand into the jar, filling all the remaining spaces. He turned to his students and said, "This jar represents your life. The rocks are your fundamental beliefs, the pebbles your values, and the sand is everything else. If you put the sand in first, there's no room for the rocks and pebbles. Your fundamental beliefs and values must come first; otherwise, your life will be out of balance."

Beloved brothers and sisters in Christ,

As we journey through the Third Week of Advent, we confront a Gospel passage from Matthew that might appear confrontational in tone. In it, the chief priests and elders of the people question Jesus about the source of His authority. His skillful and thought-provoking response places the questioners in a quandary. They find themselves unable to answer His question regarding John the Baptist's baptism, thereby leaving their own question unanswered.

This episode raises profound reflections on the nature and source of genuine authority. Like the philosopher's jar, it asks us to consider what we place at the center of our lives. Is it God's will and divine authority, represented by the rocks, or do we allow other concerns—the pebbles and the sand—to claim that space?

St. Thomas Aquinas, the great theologian, emphasized that all genuine authority comes from God and directs us towards the ultimate good. This should be the rock in our jar, the cornerstone of our lives. Any authority that does not align itself with this supreme and divine rule must be examined and, if found wanting, must give way.

The religious leaders in the Gospel failed to recognize the divine authority in Jesus and even in John the Baptist because they had filled their jars with sand and pebbles—human traditions, political concerns, and personal agendas. How often do we find ourselves in a similar situation? How often do we allow the sand and pebbles of worldly concerns to occupy the space that should be reserved for the rocks of divine will and grace?

As we light the third Advent candle, symbolizing joy, let us reflect on the source of our true joy. It isn't found in asserting our own authority or in outsmarting others, but in surrendering to God's divine authority, in submitting our wills to the loving and eternal will of the Father.

In this sacred season of Advent, let us rearrange the jars of our lives. Let us place the rocks of faith, hope, and love first, filling the spaces around them with the pebbles of virtuous living and leaving the sand of worldly concerns to occupy only the space that remains.

May the Lord bless us with the wisdom to recognize His divine authority in our lives, the courage to submit to it, and the joy that comes from a life well-ordered in His grace. Amen.

PRAYER:

Heavenly Father,

As we meditate on today's Gospel from Matthew, we are reminded of the critical question concerning authority, a question posed not merely to challenge Your Son but also to invite us to deeper contemplation. We come before You today, asking for the grace to recognize true authority, which comes solely from You.

Saint Augustine once said, "True wisdom is to know what is eternal and not to strive for things that are temporal." Grant us the wisdom to prioritize the eternal rocks of our faith—the indomitable truths of Your love and grace—above the pebbles and sand of earthly concerns. As we move through this season of Advent, help us discern what is of lasting value, aligning ourselves more fully with Your will and Your word.

In a world that often questions Your existence, Your love, and Your authority, arm us with the humble courage to stand as witnesses to Your eternal truths. Just as Your Son Jesus Christ confounded the chief priests and elders with His divine wisdom, may we, too, be instruments in bringing the light of Your truth to the dark corners of confusion, skepticism, and unbelief.

We pray that our lives may be a living testimony to Your eternal authority, so that others may come to know You and live according to Your will. Incline our hearts to seek Your face always, to listen to Your voice, and to act in accordance with Your divine commands, that we may find everlasting joy and peace.

As we journey closer to the celebration of Your Son's birth, may our hearts be attuned to the melody of Your divine authority, and may our lives be an anthem of love, sung in perfect harmony with Your will.

We offer this prayer through Christ, our Lord, who lives and reigns with You and the unity of the Holy Spirit, one God, forever and ever. Amen.

TUESDAY OF THE THIRD WEEK OF ADVENT

READING 1

ZEP 3:1-2, 9-13

Thus says the LORD:
Woe to the city, rebellious and polluted,
to the tyrannical city!
She hears no voice,
accepts no correction;
In the LORD she has not trusted,
to her God she has not drawn near.
For then I will change and purify
the lips of the peoples,
That they all may call upon the name of the LORD,
to serve him with one accord;
From beyond the rivers of Ethiopia
and as far as the recesses of the North,
they shall bring me offerings.
On that day
You need not be ashamed
of all your deeds,
your rebellious actions against me;
For then will I remove from your midst
the proud braggarts,
And you shall no longer exalt yourself
on my holy mountain.
But I will leave as a remnant in your midst
a people humble and lowly,
Who shall take refuge in the name of the LORD:
the remnant of Israel.
They shall do no wrong
and speak no lies;
Nor shall there be found in their mouths

a deceitful tongue;
They shall pasture and couch their flocks
with none to disturb them..

The word of the Lord.

RESPONSORIAL PSALM

PS 34:2-3, 6-7, 17-18, 19 AND 23

R. (7a) The Lord hears the cry of the poor.

I will bless the LORD at all times;
his praise shall be ever in my mouth.
Let my soul glory in the LORD;
the lowly will hear me and be glad.

R. The Lord hears the cry of the poor.

Look to him that you may be radiant with joy,
and your faces may not blush with shame.
When the poor one called out, the LORD heard,
and from all his distress he saved him.

R. The Lord hears the cry of the poor.

The LORD confronts the evildoers,
to destroy remembrance of them from the earth.
When the just cry out, the LORD hears them,
and from all their distress he rescues them.

R. The Lord hears the cry of the poor.
The LORD is close to the brokenhearted;
and those who are crushed in spirit he saves.
The LORD redeems the lives of his servants;
no one incurs guilt who takes refuge in him.

R. The Lord hears the cry of the poor.

ALLELUIA

R. Alleluia, alleluia.
Come, O Lord, do not delay;
forgive the sins of your people.
R. Alleluia, alleluia.

GOSPEL

MT 21:28-32

Jesus said to the chief priests and the elders of the people:
"What is your opinion?
A man had two sons.
He came to the first and said,
'Son, go out and work in the vineyard today.'
The son said in reply, 'I will not,'
but afterwards he changed his mind and went.
The man came to the other son and gave the same order.
He said in reply, 'Yes, sir,' but did not go.
Which of the two did his father's will?"
They answered, "The first."
Jesus said to them, "Amen, I say to you,
tax collectors and prostitutes
are entering the Kingdom of God before you.
When John came to you in the way of righteousness,
you did not believe him;
but tax collectors and prostitutes did.
Yet even when you saw that,
you did not later change your minds and believe him."

Brothers and sisters, the Gospel of the Lord.

HOMILY:

In a quaint European village, a young artist was commissioned to create a statue for the town square. When he presented it to the villagers, the sculpture was covered in a cloth. The artist unveiled the sculpture to reveal two sides: one side was an image of a young girl, bright-eyed and full of life; the other side was that of an old woman, weary and worn by the years. The villagers were puzzled. The artist explained, "Life is made of choices. The young girl represents hope and potential, while the old woman stands for a life of missed opportunities and regrets. It's the same face but sculpted by different choices."

Dear brothers and sisters in Christ,

In today's Gospel reading from Matthew, we are presented with the Parable of the Two Sons. One son verbally refuses his father's request to go work in the vineyard but later changes his mind and obeys. The other son agrees immediately but never actually follows through.

Jesus uses this parable to emphasize the transformation of heart that is paramount in living a life aligned with God's will.

The young artist's sculpture comes to mind because it vividly captures the essence of this parable. The two faces on the sculpture symbolize the two sons—both part of the same familial legacy but differentiated by the choices they make. The son who initially refuses but later obeys can be likened to the hopeful young girl, bright-eyed and open to transformation. The other, who gives a pleasing answer but fails in action, resembles the old, weary woman—reflecting a life of missed opportunities for grace.

St. Augustine once said, "To abstain from sin when one can no longer sin is to be forsaken by sin, not to forsake it." It is never too late to turn towards righteousness. It is never too late to be the hopeful, bright-eyed young girl instead of the weary, old woman.

This advent season, as we prepare for the coming of our Lord Jesus Christ, let us ask ourselves: Which son are we? Are we quick to say 'yes' to God but slow to act, or do we sometimes falter in our commitment only to return to the path of righteousness?

The crux of the message today is transformation—the kind of transformation that only comes from an honest self-assessment and a subsequent change of heart. We should strive to align our actions with our words, knowing that the Father values a heart that is willing to change more than lips that merely utter agreements.

As we inch closer to the commemoration of the Savior's birth, let us welcome Him with hearts transformed, actions verified, and spirits lifted high. May we be sons and daughters who not only say 'yes' to the Father but demonstrate that affirmation in how we live, love, and labor in His vineyard. Amen.

PRAYER:

Most Gracious Heavenly Father,

As we gather in prayer on this Advent Tuesday, our hearts are drawn to the contemplation of choices and commitment, spurred by the Parable of the Two Sons in the Gospel of Matthew. It serves as a poignant reminder that our actions must align with our words, and that genuine transformation emanates from the heart.

Lord, we acknowledge that like the sons in the parable, we too have faltered. There are times when we've declared our loyalty to Your will but have failed in our actions. There are also moments when our initial reluctance has turned into faithful obedience. Lord, in either case, we see Your mercy—ever-present, welcoming our transformation.

As St. Thomas Aquinas wisely noted, "To one who has faith, no explanation is necessary. To one without faith, no explanation is possible." Let our actions be the most resounding affirmation of our faith, needing no further explanation, and let our transformed hearts be living testimonies to Your boundless grace.

In this season of Advent, as we anticipate the arrival of Your Son, Jesus Christ, fill us with the grace of discernment and courage. Enable us to seize the daily opportunities for conversion and renewal, so that when Christ comes, He may find in us a people ready in both word and deed.

Bestow upon us the strength to be authentic disciples, not only receptive in hearing Your Word but zealous in living it out. May the joy of this season emanate not just from our lips but from the integrity of our actions, ensuring that our 'yes' to You, O Lord, is a 'yes' lived out in our lives.

We humbly offer this prayer through Your Son, our Lord Jesus Christ, who lives and reigns with You and the unity of the Holy Spirit, one God, forever and ever. Amen.

WEDNESDAY OF THE THIRD WEEK OF ADVENT

READING 1

IS 45:6C-8, 18, 21C-25

I am the LORD, there is no other;
I form the light, and create the darkness,
I make well-being and create woe;
I, the LORD, do all these things.
Let justice descend, O heavens, like dew from above,
like gentle rain let the skies drop it down.
Let the earth open and salvation bud forth;
let justice also spring up!
I, the LORD, have created this.
For thus says the LORD,
The creator of the heavens,
who is God,
The designer and maker of the earth
who established it,
Not creating it to be a waste,
but designing it be lived in:
I am the LORD, and there is no other.
Who announced this from the beginning
and foretold it from of old?
Was it not I, the LORD,
besides whom there is no other God?
There is no just and saving God but me.
Turn to me and be safe,
all you ends of the earth,
for I am God; there is no other!
By myself I swear,
uttering my just decree
and my unalterable word:
To me every knee shall bend;

by me every tongue shall swear,
Saying, "Only in the LORD
are just deeds and power.
Before him in shame shall come
all who vent their anger against him.
In the LORD shall be the vindication and the glory
of all the descendants of Israel."

The word of the Lord.

RESPONSORIAL PSALM

PS 85:9AB AND 10, 11-12, 13-14

R. (Isaiah 45:8) Let the clouds rain down the Just One, and the earth bring forth a Savior.

I will hear what God proclaims;
the LORD—for he proclaims peace to his people.
Near indeed is his salvation to those who fear him,
glory dwelling in our land.

R. Let the clouds rain down the Just One, and the earth bring forth a Savior.

Kindness and truth shall meet;
justice and peace shall kiss.
Truth shall spring out of the earth,
and justice shall look down from heaven.

R. Let the clouds rain down the Just One, and the earth bring forth a Savior.

The LORD himself will give his benefits;
our land shall yield its increase.
Justice shall walk before him,
and salvation, along the way of his steps.

R. Let the clouds rain down the Just One, and the earth bring forth a Savior.

ALLELUIA

See IS 40:9-10

R. Alleluia, alleluia.
Raise your voice and tell the Good News:
Behold, the Lord GOD comes with power.
R. Alleluia, alleluia.

GOSPEL

LK 7:18B-23

At that time,
John summoned two of his disciples and sent them to the Lord to ask,
"Are you the one who is to come, or should we look for another?"
When the men came to the Lord, they said,
"John the Baptist has sent us to you to ask,
'Are you the one who is to come, or should we look for another?'"
At that time Jesus cured many of their diseases, sufferings, and evil spirits;
he also granted sight to many who were blind.
And Jesus said to them in reply,
"Go and tell John what you have seen and heard:
the blind regain their sight,
the lame walk,
lepers are cleansed,
the deaf hear, the dead are raised,
the poor have the good news proclaimed to them.
And blessed is the one who takes no offense at me."

Brothers and sisters, the Gospel of the Lord.

HOMILY:

Once upon a time, a renowned violinist was scheduled to perform in a small town. Tickets were sold out weeks in advance. Finally, the night came, and the concert hall was filled to the brim with expectant people. When the violinist started playing, the audience was captivated. But in the middle of a particularly difficult piece, a string on his violin snapped. The audience gasped, but the violinist continued to play, improvising beautifully. After the performance, he was asked how he managed to continue so seamlessly. He replied, "It's not the broken string that determines the music's quality; it's how you play with what you've got left."

Dear brothers and sisters in Christ,

Today's Gospel from Luke speaks of John the Baptist sending his disciples to inquire if Jesus is indeed "the one who is to come." Our Lord answers not with a simple affirmation but by pointing to the signs and wonders that accompany His ministry— the blind regain their sight, the lame walk, and the poor have the Good News proclaimed to them.

Just like the violinist who continued to produce beautiful music despite the broken string, Jesus shows us that His messianic identity is not necessarily what people expected, but it is authentically transformative. His miracles are His melody, a divine composition that changes lives and heals souls.

St. Teresa of Avila once said, "Christ has no body now but yours. No hands, no feet on earth but yours. Yours are the eyes through which He looks compassion on this world." We are called to continue the transformative mission of Christ, to be His hands, His feet, and His voice in this world.

We can often find ourselves confined by our expectations, whether it's what we expect of ourselves, others, or even God. The message today challenges us to go beyond our expectations and to see the transformative power of God's grace, even when it isn't packaged the way we might have imagined. Just like the broken string didn't hinder the music, our imperfections shouldn't hinder us from carrying out God's work.

As we prepare ourselves in this blessed season of Advent, let us remember that we are God's instruments. We might not be perfect; we might even have a few 'broken strings,' but God can still create a beautiful melody with us. It's not about what we lack but how well we allow God to play through us.

So, let us approach the celebration of Christ's birth with a sense of purpose and anticipation, knowing that in Him, all things are made new, even the unexpected and imperfect parts of our lives. Amen.

PRAYER:

Heavenly Father,

Today, we reflect upon the Gospel according to Luke, wherein John the Baptist, though confined within prison walls, seeks to know if Jesus is the One who was promised, the One for whom the world has been waiting. Our Savior's reply is a litany of actions: the blind see, the lame walk, the dead are raised, and the Good News is delivered to the poor.

Almighty God, as we prepare our hearts and minds this Advent, fortify our faith to recognize the manifold ways in which You manifest Your love and power in our lives. In a world that often questions Your existence or needs proof of Your might, help us to be living testimonies of Your transformative grace.

Like St. Augustine, who found rest only when he found You, may our restless hearts also find solace in Your works. Open our spiritual eyes to see the miracles in everyday life: a comforting word, a healing touch, a moment of clarity, or the grace to persevere. May these be the signs that strengthen our belief and invigorate our spirits.

We pray especially for those who find it difficult to see Your presence in their lives, for those shackled by doubt, or burdened by suffering or despair. May the witness of our faith serve as a beacon, illuminating their path towards You, the source of all hope and joy.

In this journey of Advent, let us be ever mindful of Your power to make all things new. Even when circumstances seem dim, remind us that the light of Christ dispels all darkness and that our greatest testimonies often emerge from our deepest trials.

We offer this prayer through Jesus Christ, Your Son, who lives and reigns with You and the unity of the Holy Spirit, one God, forever and ever. Amen.

THURSDAY OF THE THIRD WEEK IN ADVENT

READING 1

Is 54:1-10

Raise a glad cry, you barren one who did not bear,
  Break forth in jubilant song, you who were not in labor,
For more numerous are the children of the deserted wife
  than the children of her who has a husband,
  says the Lord.
Enlarge the space for your tent,
  spread out your tent cloths unsparingly;
  lengthen your ropes and make firm your stakes.
For you shall spread abroad to the right and to the left;
  your descendants shall dispossess the nations
  and shall people the desolate cities.
Fear not, you shall not be put to shame;
  you need not blush, for you shall not be disgraced.
The shame of your youth you shall forget,
  the reproach of your widowhood no longer remember.
For he who has become your husband is your Maker;
  his name is the Lord of hosts;
Your redeemer is the Holy One of Israel,
  called God of all the earth.
The Lord calls you back,
  like a wife forsaken and grieved in spirit,
A wife married in youth and then cast off,
  says your God.
For a brief moment I abandoned you,
  but with great tenderness I will take you back.
In an outburst of wrath, for a moment
  I hid my face from you;
But with enduring love I take pity on you,
  says the Lord, your redeemer.

This is for me like the days of Noah,
   when I swore that the waters of Noah
   should never again deluge the earth;
So I have sworn not to be angry with you,
   or to rebuke you.
Though the mountains leave their place
   and the hills be shaken,
My love shall never leave you
   nor my covenant of peace be shaken,
   says the Lord, who has mercy on you.

The word of the Lord.

RESPONSORIAL PSALM

30:2 and 4, 5-6, 11-12a and 13b

R. (2a) I will praise you, Lord, for you have rescued me.

I will extol you, O Lord, for you drew me clear
   and did not let my enemies rejoice over me.
O Lord, you brought me up from the nether world;
   you preserved me from among those going down into the pit.

R. I will praise you, Lord, for you have rescued me.

Sing praise to the Lord, you his faithful ones,
   and give thanks to his holy name.
For his anger lasts but a moment;
   a lifetime, his good will.
At nightfall, weeping enters in,
   but with the dawn, rejoicing.

R. I will praise you, Lord, for you have rescued me.

"Hear, O Lord, and have pity on me;
   O Lord, be my helper."
You changed my mourning into dancing;
   O Lord, my God, forever will I give you thanks.

R. I will praise you, Lord, for you have rescued me.

ALLELUIA

Luke 3:4, 6

R. Alleluia, alleluia.
Prepare the way of the Lord, make straight his paths:
All flesh shall see the salvation of God.
R. Alleluia, alleluia.

GOSPEL

Lk 7:24-30

When the messengers of John the Baptist had left,
Jesus began to speak to the crowds about John.
"What did you go out to the desert to see -- a reed swayed by the wind?
Then what did you go out to see?
Someone dressed in fine garments?
Those who dress luxuriously and live sumptuously
are found in royal palaces.
Then what did you go out to see?
A prophet? Yes, I tell you, and more than a prophet.
This is the one about whom Scripture says:
    Behold, I am sending my messenger ahead of you,
    he will prepare your way before you.
I tell you,
among those born of women, no one is greater than John;
yet the least in the Kingdom of God is greater than he."
(All the people who listened, including the tax collectors,
who were baptized with the baptism of John,
acknowledged the righteousness of God;
but the Pharisees and scholars of the law,
who were not baptized by him,
rejected the plan of God for themselves.)

Brothers and sisters, the Gospel of the Lord.

HOMILY:

In a quaint European village lived a clockmaker renowned for his skill. His mechanical clocks were the pride of the community, keeping impeccable time and ringing melodious chimes. As years went by, digital clocks became popular, and people started to dismiss his craft as outdated. One winter, a severe storm caused a power outage, rendering all the digital clocks useless. However, the clockmaker's mechanical clocks continued to tick and chime, serving as a timely reminder that sometimes what is considered "old" may possess timeless value.

Dear brothers and sisters in Christ,

Today's Gospel from Luke enlightens us on the uniqueness and mission of John the Baptist. When the disciples of John report back to their master about Jesus, the people listening begin to ponder John's role. Jesus praises John as "more than a prophet" and acknowledges that he is the one preparing the way for the Lord.

This is an apt occasion to consider the lasting significance of tradition, illustrated beautifully by the story of the village clockmaker. In a world enamored with the new, the latest, and the instantly gratifying, there exists a timeless wisdom in tradition, much like the clockmaker's mechanical clocks that withstood the power outage.

John the Baptist can be seen as one such "mechanical clock" in the Gospel—rooted in tradition, grounded in the prophecies of old, yet perfectly attuned to the needs of the present moment. He served a pivotal role, heralding the coming of Christ. Despite being seen by some as archaic or out of touch, his message was not just timely but timeless, and it prepared the hearts of the people to recognize Jesus when He came.

St. Augustine once said, "The new is in the old concealed; the old is in the new revealed." The tradition of the prophets found its culmination in John, and John himself pointed to the new covenant in Jesus Christ. Each served its purpose in the Divine plan, just as each clock serves to tell the time, whether mechanical or digital.

As we make our journey through Advent, let us remember that our faith is both old and new. It's a living tradition that speaks to us today just as powerfully as it spoke to the generations before us. It reminds us of the need for preparation and repentance, but also of hope and joy that comes from a personal encounter with Christ.

May this season serve to deepen our appreciation for the wisdom embedded in our traditions while also opening our hearts to the ever-new possibilities offered by Christ's coming. Amen.

PRAYER:

Almighty and Merciful Father,

As we journey through this holy season of Advent, we pause today to meditate on the Gospel according to Luke, wherein Jesus extols the virtues of John the Baptist, his forerunner. John stands as a powerful testament to the strength of faith, humility, and obedience to Your divine will.

Lord, in a world that increasingly seeks the dazzling and the sensational, John the Baptist reminds us of the enduring virtues of simplicity and sincerity. As the clockmaker in our story held fast to time-honored methods, John, too, held fast to the traditions of the prophets, preparing the way for Your Son, our Savior.

As we count down the days to the celebration of Christ's birth, we pray that You endow us with the same unwavering spirit that animated John. May we become heralds in our own ways, pointing others to Christ by the witness of our lives. Help us to appreciate the depth and richness of the faith handed down to us, seeing in it not an outdated relic but a fountain of eternal truths.

O God, grant us the grace to discern the signs of the times through the lens of faith, remaining rooted in the wisdom of tradition while being open to the freshness of Your Spirit. With humility and obedience, may we participate in Your grand design, as John did, preparing the way for the experience of Christ in our hearts and in our world.

We pray this through Christ, our Lord, who lives and reigns with You and the unity of the Holy Spirit, one God, forever and ever.
Amen.

FRIDAY OF THE THIRD WEEK IN ADVENT

READING 1

Is 56:1-3a, 6-8

Thus says the LORD:
Observe what is right, do what is just;
for my salvation is about to come,
my justice, about to be revealed.
Blessed is the man who does this,
the son of man who holds to it;
Who keeps the sabbath free from profanation,
and his hand from any evildoing.
Let not the foreigner say,
when he would join himself to the LORD,
"The LORD will surely exclude me from his people."

The foreigners who join themselves to the LORD,
ministering to him,
Loving the name of the LORD,
and becoming his servants—
All who keep the sabbath free from profanation
and hold to my covenant,
Them I will bring to my holy mountain
and make joyful in my house of prayer;
Their burnt offerings and sacrifices
will be acceptable on my altar,
For my house shall be called
a house of prayer for all peoples.
Thus says the Lord GOD,
who gathers the dispersed of Israel:
Others will I gather to him
besides those already gathered.
The word of the Lord.

RESPONSORIAL PSALM

Ps 67:2-3, 5, 7-8

R. (4) O God, let all the nations praise you!

May God have pity on us and bless us;
may he let his face shine upon us.
So may your way be known upon earth;
among all nations, your salvation.

R. O God, let all the nations praise you!

May the nations be glad and exult
because you rule the peoples in equity;
the nations on the earth you guide.

R. O God, let all the nations praise you!

The earth has yielded its fruits;
God, our God, has blessed us.
May God bless us,
and may all the ends of the earth fear him!

R. O God, let all the nations praise you!

ALLELUIA

R. Alleluia, alleluia.
Come, Lord, bring us your peace
that we may rejoice before you with a perfect heart.
R. Alleluia, alleluia.

GOSPEL

Jn 5:33-36

Jesus said to the Jews:
"You sent emissaries to John, and he testified to the truth.
I do not accept testimony from a human being,
but I say this so that you may be saved.
John was a burning and shining lamp,
and for a while you were content to rejoice in his light.
But I have testimony greater than John's.
The works that the Father gave me to accomplish,
these works that I perform testify on my behalf
that the Father has sent me."

Brothers and sisters, the Gospel of the Lord.

HOMILY:

In a small, sleepy town, there was a lighthouse that stood on a cliff overlooking the ocean. It had been there for generations, faithfully guiding ships to safe harbor. One day, a young man moved to town and found the lighthouse to be an antiquated notion. "Why not use GPS and modern technology?" he would often say. The townspeople explained that the lighthouse served as a backup, something trustworthy when all else failed. One foggy night, a technical glitch caused the GPS systems on a cargo ship to fail, and it was the timeless beacon from the lighthouse that guided the ship to safety.

Dear faithful in Christ,

As we delve into today's Gospel from John, we are invited to ponder upon the testimony of John the Baptist concerning Jesus. John himself has been a beacon, a spiritual lighthouse, guiding the people towards the Messiah. Yet, he points out that his testimony is not the main focus; rather, the works that Jesus does are the true and perfect testament to His divinity.

This brings to mind the story of the lighthouse. Much like the lighthouse serves as a guide but is not the ultimate destination, John the Baptist directs us towards Jesus. His mission is not to glorify himself, but to illuminate the path towards Christ, who is the true Light. His testimony serves to reinforce what is already apparent through the miraculous deeds performed by Jesus.

Again as St. Thomas Aquinas once said, "To one who has faith, no explanation is necessary. To one without faith, no explanation is possible." The miracles of Christ, the fulfillment of prophecies, and the continuation of His Church—all these are testimonies that require no further evidence for those who have faith.

However, we live in an age where the credibility of spiritual testimonies is often questioned. In this context, we must turn our eyes to the enduring nature of faith. Just as the townspeople stood by the lighthouse, knowing its time-tested reliability, we too should stand by our faith, recognizing its eternal and unchanging nature.

As we progress through Advent, let us remember the role of testimonies in our lives—not merely as standalone affirmations but as signposts directing us towards a deeper truth. The testimony of John the Baptist and the miracles of Christ are lighthouses on our spiritual journey, guiding us towards safe harbor in God.

In the midst of life's complexities, these testimonies invite us to repose in the simple yet profound truth: Christ has come, is present, and will come again. Let us prepare our hearts to receive Him anew this Advent season. Amen.

PRAYER:

Heavenly Father, Giver of Light and Truth,

On this day, we reflect upon the Gospel according to John, wherein the role of John the Baptist as a witness to Your Son, Jesus Christ, is highlighted. As the Baptist was a lamp shining in the darkness, leading people towards the true Light of the world, we are reminded of our own calling to bear witness to Christ.

Father, today we recall the story of the lighthouse, which, despite its antiquity, remains an unfailing guide for ships lost in the fog. In a similar manner, the testimony of John the Baptist has withstood the test of time, forever pointing us toward Your Son. Let us too be lighthouses in our modern world—beacons of faith, hope, and charity—despite the fog of doubt and the storms of despair that cloud human hearts.

We pray, O Lord, that our lives may become testimonies as compelling as those performed by Jesus, which John the Baptist declared were greater attestations of His divinity than any words could provide. Grant us the courage to live our faith openly and lovingly, that we might draw others closer to You.

O Divine Artisan, we ask that You continue to shape and mold us in the way of holiness, so that we may become worthy vessels of Your truth. In our actions, conversations, and even in our silences, let Your love radiate, bearing witness to the saving power of Your Son, Jesus Christ.

May this Advent season deepen our desire to live authentic lives, guided by the teachings of Your Church, and inspired by the lives of the saints who have shown us the way to true discipleship.

We pray this in the name of Your Son, our Lord Jesus Christ, who lives and reigns with You and the unity of the Holy Spirit, one God, forever and ever. Amen.

THE WEEKDAYS OF ADVENT (DECEMBER 17)

READING I

Gn 49:2, 8-10

Jacob called his sons and said to them:
"Assemble and listen, sons of Jacob,
　listen to Israel, your father.
"You, Judah, shall your brothers praise
　–your hand on the neck of your enemies;
　the sons of your father shall bow down to you.
Judah, like a lion's whelp,
　you have grown up on prey, my son.
He crouches like a lion recumbent,
　the king of beasts–who would dare rouse him?
The scepter shall never depart from Judah,
　or the mace from between his legs,
While tribute is brought to him,
　and he receives the people's homage."

The word of the Lord.

RESPONSORIAL PSALM

72:1-2, 3-4ab, 7-8, 17

R. (see 7) Justice shall flourish in his time, and fullness of peace forever.

O God, with your judgment endow the king,
   and with your justice, the king's son;
He shall govern your people with justice
   and your afflicted ones with judgment.

R. Justice shall flourish in his time, and fullness of peace forever.
The mountains shall yield peace for the people,
   and the hills justice.
He shall defend the afflicted among the people,
   save the children of the poor.

R. Justice shall flourish in his time, and fullness of peace forever.

Justice shall flower in his days,
   and profound peace, till the moon be no more.
May he rule from sea to sea,
   and from the River to the ends of the earth.

R. Justice shall flourish in his time, and fullness of peace forever.

May his name be blessed forever;
   as long as the sun his name shall remain.
In him shall all the tribes of the earth be blessed;
   all the nations shall proclaim his happiness.

R. Justice shall flourish in his time, and fullness of peace forever.

ALLELUIA

R. Alleluia, alleluia.
O Wisdom of our God Most High,
guiding creation with power and love:
come to teach us the path of knowledge!
R. Alleluia, alleluia.

GOSPEL

Mt 1:1-17

The book of the genealogy of Jesus Christ,
the son of David, the son of Abraham.
Abraham became the father of Isaac,
Isaac the father of Jacob,
Jacob the father of Judah and his brothers.
Judah became the father of Perez and Zerah,
whose mother was Tamar.
Perez became the father of Hezron,
Hezron the father of Ram,
Ram the father of Amminadab.
Amminadab became the father of Nahshon,
Nahshon the father of Salmon,
Salmon the father of Boaz,
whose mother was Rahab.
Boaz became the father of Obed,
whose mother was Ruth.
Obed became the father of Jesse,
Jesse the father of David the king.
David became the father of Solomon,
whose mother had been the wife of Uriah.
Solomon became the father of Rehoboam,
Rehoboam the father of Abijah,
Abijah the father of Asaph.
Asaph became the father of Jehoshaphat,
Jehoshaphat the father of Joram,
Joram the father of Uzziah.
Uzziah became the father of Jotham,
Jotham the father of Ahaz,
Ahaz the father of Hezekiah.

Hezekiah became the father of Manasseh,
Manasseh the father of Amos,
Amos the father of Josiah.
Josiah became the father of Jechoniah and his brothers
at the time of the Babylonian exile.
After the Babylonian exile,
Jechoniah became the father of Shealtiel,
Shealtiel the father of Zerubbabel,
Zerubbabel the father of Abiud.
Abiud became the father of Eliakim,
Eliakim the father of Azor,
Azor the father of Zadok.
Zadok became the father of Achim,
Achim the father of Eliud,
Eliud the father of Eleazar.
Eleazar became the father of Matthan,
Matthan the father of Jacob,
Jacob the father of Joseph, the husband of Mary.
Of her was born Jesus who is called the Christ.
Thus the total number of generations
from Abraham to David
is fourteen generations;
from David to the Babylonian exile, fourteen generations;
from the Babylonian exile to the Christ,
fourteen generations.

Brothers and sisters, the Gospel of the Lord.

HOMILY:

In a quaint little village, there was an old library that seemed to have been forgotten by time. Its shelves were laden with dusty books, many of which were genealogical records of the village families. One day, a young girl named Emily wandered into the library and started exploring. She stumbled upon her own family's genealogical book. As she flipped through the pages, she discovered her lineage traced back to one of the village's founding figures. A sense of awe and pride enveloped her. It wasn't just the names in the book; it was the narrative of resilience, sacrifice, and love that had allowed her to be who she was today.

Dearest brothers and sisters in Christ,

As we mark today, December 17th, we shift our Advent focus more explicitly towards the Nativity of our Lord. The Gospel according to Matthew starts with a genealogy, a seemingly dry list of names that trace the lineage of Jesus Christ back to Abraham. One might ask, why is this genealogical account important? Just as young Emily discovered the richness of her heritage in that old library, so too do we uncover the depth and grandeur of God's unfolding plan for humanity in this list of names.

Indeed, the genealogy of Jesus is not just a list; it is a tapestry woven through generations, integrating different threads of sinners, saints, kings, and commoners. People like Rahab, a Canaanite; Ruth, a Moabite; and David, a man after God's own heart yet flawed in many ways, are all part of this intricate design. Each name represents a story, a lesson, and most importantly, a divine orchestration leading to the birth of our Savior.

The philosopher Søren Kierkegaard once said, "Life can only be understood backward, but it must be lived forwards." It's a wisdom that seems particularly fitting today. The genealogy demonstrates the extraordinary power of God to write straight with crooked lines, to bring about perfect ends through imperfect means.

St. Augustine eloquently reminds us that "God is always trying to give good things to us, but our hands are too full to receive them." This Advent, as we prepare to celebrate the birth of Christ, let us make space in our hands and our hearts. As we continue to delve deeper into our faith, let our lives be a testament to God's enduring love, just as the genealogy of Jesus showcases the richness and complexity of God's providential care throughout the ages.

So, let us come before the Lord with humble hearts, acknowledging the lineage from which we spiritually descend—a lineage that culminates in the person of Jesus Christ, the Alpha and the Omega, the beginning and the end. Amen.

PRAYER:

Almighty God, Author of all history and Sustainer of our lineage, spiritual and biological,

As we gather on this weekday of Advent, December 17th, our hearts turn toward the immanent celebration of the birth of Your beloved Son, Jesus Christ. Today's Gospel takes us through a genealogical journey, spanning from Abraham to Joseph, revealing the divine tapestry You have woven through generations.

Lord, just as every name in the lineage of Christ had its purpose, we recognize that we, too, have a unique purpose in the ongoing story of salvation. Inscribe upon our hearts the profound truth that we are links in a chain, a chain that is neither accidental nor arbitrary but a sequence in Your divine plan.

We are reminded today of St. Teresa of Ávila, who said, "All troubles of the Church come from people thinking they are something." On this Advent day, let us be humbled, seeing ourselves as small yet significant threads in the expansive tapestry of Your grand design. Grant us the grace to see our own lives in connection with the saints and sinners of old, and to appreciate the collective journey that has shaped our faith today.

Father, help us to learn from the righteous and flawed characters in Jesus' genealogy, understanding that You can use us irrespective of our imperfections to accomplish Your will. Fill us with the same faith that guided Abraham, the same courage that empowered David, and the same resilience that characterized Ruth.

As we look forward to celebrating the birth of Jesus, let the rich heritage of faith be our guide and inspiration. Fortify us, O Lord, to play our part faithfully, that we may be worthy to share in the inheritance promised to us through Your Son, Jesus Christ.

Heavenly Father, may our preparation this Advent be pleasing to You, as we await with joyous anticipation the coming of our Savior, Jesus Christ, in whose name we offer this prayer. Amen.

THE WEEKDAYS OF ADVENT (DECEMBER 18)

READING 1

Jer 23:5-8

Behold, the days are coming, says the LORD,
when I will raise up a righteous shoot to David;
As king he shall reign and govern wisely,
he shall do what is just and right in the land.
In his days Judah shall be saved,
Israel shall dwell in security.
This is the name they give him:
"The LORD our justice."

Therefore, the days will come, says the LORD,
when they shall no longer say, "As the LORD lives,
who brought the children of Israel out of the land of Egypt";
but rather, "As the LORD lives,
who brought the descendants of the house of Israel
up from the land of the north"–
and from all the lands to which I banished them;
they shall again live on their own land.

The word of the Lord.

RESPONSORIAL PSALM

Ps 72:1-2, 12-13, 18-19

R. (see 7) Justice shall flourish in his time, and fullness of peace forever.

O God, with your judgment endow the king,
and with your justice, the king's son;
He shall govern your people with justice
and your afflicted ones with judgment.

R. Justice shall flourish in his time, and fullness of peace forever.

For he shall rescue the poor when he cries out,
and the afflicted when he has no one to help him.
He shall have pity for the lowly and the poor;
the lives of the poor he shall save.

R. Justice shall flourish in his time, and fullness of peace forever.

Blessed be the LORD, the God of Israel,
who alone does wondrous deeds.
And blessed forever be his glorious name;
may the whole earth be filled with his glory.

R. Justice shall flourish in his time, and fullness of peace forever.

ALLELUIA

R. Alleluia, alleluia.
O Leader of the House of Israel,
giver of the Law to Moses on Sinai:
come to rescue us with your mighty power!
R. Alleluia, alleluia.

GOSPEL

Mt 1:18-25

This is how the birth of Jesus Christ came about.
When his mother Mary was betrothed to Joseph,
but before they lived together,
she was found with child through the Holy Spirit.
Joseph her husband, since he was a righteous man,
yet unwilling to expose her to shame,
decided to divorce her quietly.
Such was his intention when, behold,
the angel of the Lord appeared to him in a dream and said,
"Joseph, son of David,
do not be afraid to take Mary your wife into your home.
For it is through the Holy Spirit
that this child has been conceived in her.
She will bear a son and you are to name him Jesus,
because he will save his people from their sins."
All this took place to fulfill
what the Lord had said through the prophet:

Behold, the virgin shall be with child and bear a son,
and they shall name him Emmanuel,

which means "God is with us."
When Joseph awoke,
he did as the angel of the Lord had commanded him
and took his wife into his home.
He had no relations with her until she bore a son,
and he named him Jesus.

Brothers and sisters, the Gospel of the Lord.

HOMILY:

A craftsman named Robert spent months meticulously building a wooden crib for his soon-to-be-born grandchild. Each piece was carved with love and assembled with skill. The crib was more than just a bed; it was a heritage, a manifestation of love, destined to be a family heirloom. When it was finally completed, he hesitated, contemplating whether it was "worthy" for such an important role. Finally, his wife gently reminded him, "Sometimes, love is about having the faith to offer what you can, trusting that it will be enough."

Dear brothers and sisters in Christ,

Today, we find ourselves further into the season of Advent, a season characterized by longing, preparation, and ever-growing hope. The Gospel of Matthew narrates to us the events surrounding the conception and birth of Jesus, with an emphasis on Joseph's role. St. Joseph, betrothed to Mary, finds her to be with child through the Holy Spirit. What we witness here is a profound lesson on trust, obedience, and God's intricate design unfolding in the lives of everyday people.

St. Joseph is often overshadowed by the resplendent figures of Mary and Jesus, yet he provides a quiet testament to faith in action. Facing a situation that defies human understanding, he chooses to believe in divine providence rather than societal norms. His faith is an active faith, fortified by his openness to divine messages conveyed through dreams. How often do we, when faced with inexplicable events in our lives, default to skepticism rather than faith?

The story of Joseph is a remarkable illustration of this wisdom. Joseph had every worldly reason to abandon Mary, but he chose to embrace the inscrutable designs of God. He wasn't merely accepting the situation; he was actively taking on a role in the salvation story, akin to our craftsman Robert, who built not just a crib but a legacy.

This narrative invites us to reflect on our own lives. How often are we faced with circumstances that challenge our understanding and test our faith? Do we react with doubt and trepidation, or do we embrace these instances as opportunities for grace and divine intervention? St. Joseph's story teaches us that surrender to God does not signify defeat; rather, it signifies a victorious partnership with the divine.

St. Augustine once said, "God provides the wind, but man must raise the sails." Joseph raised his sails high, surrendering to the course charted by God. As we journey further into Advent, let this be our prayer and aim—to raise our sails, to trust in the divine wind, to be active participants in God's marvelous plan for salvation.

In faith and obedience, we prepare not just our homes but our hearts for the coming of our Savior, Jesus Christ. May we, like Joseph, find the courage to embrace God's plan for us, even when it contradicts our expectations or defies our understanding. Amen.

PRAYER:

Heavenly Father, during this blessed season of Advent, we come before You with hearts filled with awe and expectation. Today, we reflect on the Gospel of Matthew, where we witness the obedience and steadfast faith of St. Joseph. His willingness to accept Your divine plan, even in the face of uncertainty and societal judgment, serves as an inspiration for all of us.

As we prepare for the miraculous birth of Your Son, Jesus Christ, instill in us the same unwavering faith exhibited by St. Joseph. May his devotion remind us to be open to Your divine messages, whether they come through dreams, through the words of the Scriptures, or through the gentle nudges of the Holy Spirit in our daily lives.

Lord, grant us the courage to step out in faith when You call us, even if the path seems arduous and the future unclear. Help us to silence the clamor of the world, so that we can hear Your voice guiding us in the direction You have prepared for us. Just as Joseph served as a protective earthly father to Jesus, let us also protect and nurture the faith you have planted within us and in those we influence.

We remember the words of St. Augustine: "Trust the past to the mercy of God, the present to His love, and the future to His providence." Lord, we place our past mistakes, our current challenges, and our future uncertainties into Your capable hands. In these remaining days of Advent, prepare our hearts to receive the Christ child with pure joy and gratitude.

Through the intercession of St. Joseph, patron of fathers, workers, and the universal Church, we ask for the grace to live this Advent season in true preparation for the advent of Your Kingdom here on Earth, as it is in Heaven. Amen.

THE WEEKDAYS OF ADVENT (DECEMBER 19)

READING 1

Jgs 13:2-7, 24-25a

There was a certain man from Zorah, of the clan of the Danites,
whose name was Manoah.
His wife was barren and had borne no children.
An angel of the LORD appeared to the woman and said to her,
"Though you are barren and have had no children,
yet you will conceive and bear a son.
Now, then, be careful to take no wine or strong drink
and to eat nothing unclean.
As for the son you will conceive and bear,
no razor shall touch his head,
for this boy is to be consecrated to God from the womb.
It is he who will begin the deliverance of Israel
from the power of the Philistines."

The woman went and told her husband,
"A man of God came to me;
he had the appearance of an angel of God, terrible indeed.
I did not ask him where he came from, nor did he tell me his name.
But he said to me,
'You will be with child and will bear a son.
So take neither wine nor strong drink, and eat nothing unclean.
For the boy shall be consecrated to God from the womb,
until the day of his death.'"

The woman bore a son and named him Samson.
The boy grew up and the LORD blessed him;
the Spirit of the LORD stirred him.

The word of the Lord.

RESPONSORIAL PSALM

Ps 71:3-4a, 5-6ab, 16-17

R. (see 8) My mouth shall be filled with your praise, and I will sing your glory!

Be my rock of refuge,
a stronghold to give me safety,
for you are my rock and my fortress.
O my God, rescue me from the hand of the wicked.

R. My mouth shall be filled with your praise, and I will sing your glory!

For you are my hope, O LORD;
my trust, O God, from my youth.
On you I depend from birth;
from my mother's womb you are my strength.

R. My mouth shall be filled with your praise, and I will sing your glory!

I will treat of the mighty works of the LORD;
O God, I will tell of your singular justice.
O God, you have taught me from my youth,
and till the present I proclaim your wondrous deeds.

R. My mouth shall be filled with your praise, and I will sing your glory!

ALLELUIA

R. Alleluia, alleluia.
O Root of Jesse's stem,
sign of God's love for all his people:
come to save us without delay!
R. Alleluia, alleluia.

GOSPEL

Lk 1:5-25

In the days of Herod, King of Judea,
there was a priest named Zechariah
of the priestly division of Abijah;
his wife was from the daughters of Aaron,
and her name was Elizabeth.
Both were righteous in the eyes of God,
observing all the commandments
and ordinances of the Lord blamelessly.
But they had no child, because Elizabeth was barren
and both were advanced in years.

Once when he was serving as priest
in his division's turn before God,
according to the practice of the priestly service,
he was chosen by lot
to enter the sanctuary of the Lord to burn incense.
Then, when the whole assembly of the people was praying outside
at the hour of the incense offering,
the angel of the Lord appeared to him,
standing at the right of the altar of incense.
Zechariah was troubled by what he saw, and fear came upon him.

But the angel said to him, "Do not be afraid, Zechariah,
because your prayer has been heard.
Your wife Elizabeth will bear you a son,
and you shall name him John.
And you will have joy and gladness,
and many will rejoice at his birth,
for he will be great in the sight of the Lord.

He will drink neither wine nor strong drink.
He will be filled with the Holy Spirit even from his mother's womb,
and he will turn many of the children of Israel
to the Lord their God.
He will go before him in the spirit and power of Elijah
to turn the hearts of fathers toward children
and the disobedient to the understanding of the righteous,
to prepare a people fit for the Lord."

Then Zechariah said to the angel,
"How shall I know this?
For I am an old man, and my wife is advanced in years."
And the angel said to him in reply,
"I am Gabriel, who stand before God.
I was sent to speak to you and to announce to you this good news.
But now you will be speechless and unable to talk
until the day these things take place,
because you did not believe my words,
which will be fulfilled at their proper time."
Meanwhile the people were waiting for Zechariah
and were amazed that he stayed so long in the sanctuary.
But when he came out, he was unable to speak to them,
and they realized that he had seen a vision in the sanctuary.
He was gesturing to them but remained mute.

Then, when his days of ministry were completed, he went home.

After this time his wife Elizabeth conceived,
and she went into seclusion for five months, saying,
"So has the Lord done for me at a time when he has seen fit
to take away my disgrace before others."

Brothers and sisters, the Gospel of the Lord.

HOMILY:

In the times of yore, there was a village where people rarely had children after reaching a certain age. Yet, in this very village lived an elderly couple who never gave up hope. Each day, the couple would visit the temple and pray for a child, despite their advanced age and the skepticism of their community. The villagers considered their continued prayers almost foolish and thought they should resign themselves to God's will. However, one day, an itinerant sage came to the village and, having heard their story, told the couple that sometimes miracles are waiting for the right moment to appear. Not long after, the couple was blessed with a child. They named him "Hope," to signify that one should never give up on God's mercy and miracles.

Beloved in Christ, as we delve into the richness of today's Gospel from (Luke 1:5-25,) we find the story of Zechariah and Elizabeth, a righteous but barren couple. This narrative holds a special resonance during this season of Advent, a season marked by hope, expectation, and divine revelation.

Much like the elderly couple in the story, Zechariah and Elizabeth also found themselves wrestling with the sorrow of childlessness, a condition often perceived as a curse in their social context. Yet, they remained steadfast in their faith and "were righteous in the sight of God, observing all the Lord's commands and decrees blamelessly."

In the case of Zechariah, an extraordinary thing happened while he was performing his priestly duty. An angel of the Lord appeared to him, declaring that Elizabeth would bear a son who would be named John. This child was to be great in the eyes of the Lord and would prepare the people for the coming of the Lord. This was no ordinary event; it was a divine intervention, a miracle that would change the course of their lives and the lives of all Israel.

As St. Augustine once wisely noted, "Miracles are not contrary to nature but only contrary to what we know about nature." In a sense, the life of John the Baptist was a miracle that prepared the way for the greatest miracle of all: the Incarnation of the Word of God.

Yet, even as he received this incredible news, Zechariah was struck dumb, quite literally, for his inability to immediately believe the promise delivered by the angel Gabriel. His silence until the birth of John can be seen as a contemplative pause, a reminder for us all to reflect deeply on the mysteries of God that often defy our human logic and understanding.

In this season of Advent, let us remember to make room in our lives for God's unexpected graces. Whether it is the birth of a child in seemingly impossible circumstances or the change of heart in someone we have long prayed for, miracles often come to those who wait with a faithful heart.

Dear brothers and sisters, as we approach the birth of our Savior, Jesus Christ, let us hold fast to hope, and let us never underestimate the power of God to bring life where there seems only barrenness. Let us remember that, in God's perfect timing, barrenness makes way for bounty, silence gives birth to proclamation, and human frailty is transformed by divine strength.

May the grace of the Lord fill our hearts this Advent, preparing us for the miracles that await us in the celebration of the Incarnation of our Lord and Savior, Jesus Christ. Amen.

PRAYER:

Almighty and Everlasting Father,

As we gather in Your presence this Advent season, our hearts are filled with anticipation and wonder, mindful of the miraculous stories that foreshadow the arrival of Your Son, our Lord Jesus Christ. Today, we reflect on the Gospel according to Luke, recounting the tale of Zechariah and Elizabeth, a devout couple who found favor in Your sight.

Lord, their story is a testament to Your boundless grace, a reminder that even in the wilderness of barrenness and the silence of unanswered prayers, You are actively at work. You turned their sorrow into joy, their waiting into a fulfillment beyond their imagination. Through the angel Gabriel, You heralded the coming of John the Baptist, the forerunner of our Savior, as a sign that no situation is too hopeless for Your redemptive power.

Father, we pray for those among us who, like Zechariah and Elizabeth, find themselves waiting on You, perhaps doubting whether the time for miracles has passed them by. May the hope of this Advent season penetrate the hardened corners of our hearts, enabling us to trust in Your perfect timing. May we, like Elizabeth, proclaim, "The Lord has done this for me," recognizing that even when we are silent or doubtful, You are still God, and You are good.

May this Advent season not only be a time of waiting but also a time of spiritual awakening, where the eyes of our hearts are opened to recognize Your works of mercy and grace in our lives. As we await the celebration of the birth of Jesus Christ, fill us with the same Holy Spirit that filled John the Baptist, that we may be empowered to prepare the way for Your coming into the lives of those around us.

We pray all these things in the blessed name of Your Son, Jesus Christ, through the intercession of all Your saints and the outpouring of the Holy Spirit. Amen.

THE WEEKDAYS OF ADVENT (DECEMBER 20)

READING 1

Is 7:10-14

The LORD spoke to Ahaz:
Ask for a sign from the LORD, your God;
let it be deep as the nether world, or high as the sky!
But Ahaz answered,
"I will not ask! I will not tempt the LORD!"
Then Isaiah said:
Listen, O house of David!
Is it not enough for you to weary men,
must you also weary my God?
Therefore the Lord himself will give you this sign:
the virgin shall conceive and bear a son,
and shall name him Emmanuel.

The word of the Lord.

RESPONSORIAL PSALM

Ps 24:1-2, 3-4ab, 5-6

R. (see 7c and 10b) Let the Lord enter; he is the king of glory.

The LORD's are the earth and its fullness;
the world and those who dwell in it.
For he founded it upon the seas
and established it upon the rivers.
R. Let the Lord enter; he is the king of glory.
Who can ascend the mountain of the LORD?
or who may stand in his holy place?
He whose hands are sinless, whose heart is clean,
who desires not what is vain.

R. Let the Lord enter; he is the king of glory.

He shall receive a blessing from the LORD,
a reward from God his savior.
Such is the race that seeks for him,
that seeks the face of the God of Jacob.

R. Let the Lord enter; he is the king of glory.

ALLELUIA

R. Alleluia, alleluia.
O Key of David,
opening the gates of God's eternal Kingdom:
come and free the prisoners of darkness!
R. Alleluia, alleluia.

GOSPEL

Lk 1:26-38

In the sixth month,
the angel Gabriel was sent from God
to a town of Galilee called Nazareth,
to a virgin betrothed to a man named Joseph,
of the house of David,
and the virgin's name was Mary.
And coming to her, he said,
"Hail, full of grace! The Lord is with you."
But she was greatly troubled at what was said
and pondered what sort of greeting this might be.
Then the angel said to her,
"Do not be afraid, Mary,
for you have found favor with God.
Behold, you will conceive in your womb and bear a son,
and you shall name him Jesus.
He will be great and will be called Son of the Most High,
and the Lord God will give him the throne of David his father,
and he will rule over the house of Jacob forever,
and of his Kingdom there will be no end."

But Mary said to the angel,
"How can this be,
since I have no relations with a man?"
And the angel said to her in reply,
"The Holy Spirit will come upon you,
and the power of the Most High will overshadow you.
Therefore the child to be born
will be called holy, the Son of God.
And behold, Elizabeth, your relative,
has also conceived a son in her old age,
and this is the sixth month for her who was called barren;
for nothing will be impossible for God."

Mary said, "Behold, I am the handmaid of the Lord.
May it be done to me according to your word."
Then the angel departed from her.

Brothers and sisters, the Gospel of the Lord.

HOMILY:

In the art world, there exists a masterpiece by the Baroque painter Caravaggio titled "The Annunciation." This painting is unlike many traditional depictions of the same biblical event. In it, the angel Gabriel does not appear with flamboyant wings or radiant light but comes forth as an ordinary-looking boy, seemingly interrupting the Virgin Mary, who appears contemplative, if not somewhat surprised. The scene is ordinary, yet the message is extraordinary. The painting serves as a reminder that divine intervention often takes place in the most common circumstances, disrupting the 'normal' to make way for the miraculous.

Dearly Beloved,

As we delve into the Scripture of the day, the Gospel of Luke (1:26-38,) our attention is drawn to a remarkable encounter between the angel Gabriel and the Virgin Mary—an encounter where the extraordinary infuses the ordinary, and the mundane becomes sacred. Today, we walk in the footsteps of Mary, a young woman who becomes the recipient of a divine message that will irrevocably change not only her life but also the course of human history.

At first glance, it is easy to romanticize the Annunciation as a celestial, otherworldly event, far removed from our everyday experience. Yet, when we engage more deeply with the text, we discover a young woman who is initially perplexed and troubled by Gabriel's greeting. Her confusion echoes our own when we are confronted with situations that bewilder or frighten us. Mary's first response is one of questioning: "How can this be?" This query bears witness to her human condition—a condition filled with limitations, uncertainties, and fears.

And here, in this moment of perplexity, is where the extraordinary happens. The angel Gabriel reassures Mary, "The Holy Spirit will come upon you, and the power of the Most High will overshadow you." These words serve as a profound theological declaration that God's Spirit is the active agent in our lives, capable of turning impossibility into possibility, of transforming barrenness into a life overflowing with divine grace.

Mary's fiat, her "yes" to God, serves as a lesson for us all. Her response was not blind obedience but an act of faith rooted in her relationship with God—a relationship that empowered her to participate in God's salvific plan. The theologian Karl Rahner once noted that God's self-communication is always a dialogue. Mary's "yes" echoes this dialogical nature of God's revelation, for her faith response creates the space where God can manifest His glory.

Let us take inspiration from the lives of the saints, such as St. Augustine, who discerned the voice of God amidst his own life's disarray and converted, ultimately saying "yes" to God's love. Likewise, as we journey through this season of Advent, may we be courageous enough to question, faithful enough to listen, and humble enough to say "yes" to God's plans for us—even when, especially when, those plans disrupt our understanding of 'normal'.

Advent is a season of preparation and anticipation. Like the Virgin Mary, we are each called to prepare room in the inns of our hearts, that Christ may find a dwelling place within us. Through the intercession of Mary and all the saints, may we find the courage to say "yes" to God, embracing the miraculous that is born from the ordinary.

May your Advent be a time of profound grace, joyful expectation, and deep spiritual renewal. Amen.

PRAYER:

Heavenly Father, God of Promises and Fulfillment,

As we gather in Your name, our hearts are filled with awe and reverence in this season of Advent—a season where the ordinary becomes extraordinary, a season that mirrors the miraculous events of the Annunciation. Just as You sent the angel Gabriel to Mary, we humbly ask You to send Your Spirit to us, to guide us and help us discern Your will in our lives.

Lord, we reflect on Mary's humble and willing spirit, her courageous 'yes' that paved the way for our salvation. Grant us the grace to embrace Your will with similar openness, even when faced with uncertainties or difficulties. Fill us with Your Holy Spirit, that we might trust in Your plans and believe in the miracles that unfold from a life surrendered to You.

Like Mary, may we ponder Your words in our hearts, and let our lives be a song of Magnificat, proclaiming Your greatness. Teach us to be active participants in Your saving work, willing to bear Christ into a world in desperate need of love and redemption.

Through this Advent journey, kindle within us an enduring faith, a joyful hope, and a tireless love. May the anticipation of Christ's birth fill us with renewed purpose and commitment to serve You in all that we do.

Inspired by the lives of Your saints—St. Augustine, who turned to You amidst a life of confusion, and the Blessed Virgin Mary, who embraced Your call with faith—we humbly beseech Your guidance and protection as we navigate the complexities of our modern world. Let this season be a time of spiritual preparation, of making room for Christ in the inn of our hearts, and of spreading Your message of salvation to all corners of the earth.

We ask this through Christ, our Lord, who lives and reigns with You and the unity of the Holy Spirit, one God, forever and ever. Amen.

THE WEEKDAYS OF ADVENT (DECEMBER 21)

READING 1

Sg 2:8-14

Hark! my lover–here he comes
springing across the mountains,
leaping across the hills.
My lover is like a gazelle
or a young stag.
Here he stands behind our wall,
gazing through the windows,
peering through the lattices.
My lover speaks; he says to me,
"Arise, my beloved, my dove, my beautiful one,
and come!
"For see, the winter is past,
the rains are over and gone.
The flowers appear on the earth,
the time of pruning the vines has come,
and the song of the dove is heard in our land.
The fig tree puts forth its figs,
and the vines, in bloom, give forth fragrance.
Arise, my beloved, my beautiful one,
and come!

"O my dove in the clefts of the rock,
in the secret recesses of the cliff,
Let me see you,
let me hear your voice,
For your voice is sweet,
and you are lovely."
The word of the Lord.

Or

Zep 3:14-18a

Shout for joy, O daughter Zion!
Sing joyfully, O Israel!
Be glad and exult with all your heart,
O daughter Jerusalem!
The LORD has removed the judgment against you,
he has turned away your enemies;
The King of Israel, the LORD, is in your midst,
you have no further misfortune to fear.
On that day, it shall be said to Jerusalem:
Fear not, O Zion, be not discouraged!
The LORD, your God, is in your midst,
a mighty savior;
He will rejoice over you with gladness,
and renew you in his love,
He will sing joyfully because of you,
as one sings at festivals.

RESPONSORIAL PSALM

Ps 33:2-3, 11-12, 20-21

R. (1a; 3a) Exult, you just, in the Lord! Sing to him a new song.

Give thanks to the LORD on the harp;
with the ten-stringed lyre chant his praises.
Sing to him a new song;
pluck the strings skillfully, with shouts of gladness.

R. Exult, you just, in the Lord! Sing to him a new song.

But the plan of the LORD stands forever;
the design of his heart, through all generations.
Blessed the nation whose God is the LORD,
the people he has chosen for his own inheritance.

R. Exult, you just, in the Lord! Sing to him a new song.

Our soul waits for the LORD,
who is our help and our shield,

For in him our hearts rejoice;
in his holy name we trust.

R. Exult, you just, in the Lord! Sing to him a new song.

ALLELUIA

R. Alleluia, alleluia.
O Emmanuel, our King and Giver of Law:
come to save us, Lord our God!
R. Alleluia, alleluia.

GOSPEL

Lk 1:39-45

Mary set out in those days
and traveled to the hill country in haste
to a town of Judah,
where she entered the house of Zechariah
and greeted Elizabeth.
When Elizabeth heard Mary's greeting,
the infant leaped in her womb,
and Elizabeth, filled with the Holy Spirit,
cried out in a loud voice and said,
"Most blessed are you among women,
and blessed is the fruit of your womb.
And how does this happen to me,
that the mother of my Lord should come to me?
For at the moment the sound of your greeting reached my ears,
the infant in my womb leaped for joy.
Blessed are you who believed
that what was spoken to you by the Lord
would be fulfilled."

Brothers and sisters, the Gospel of the Lord.

HOMILY:

During the early 20th century, two friends set off on an expedition to explore a remote mountain range. They were avid mountaineers, and both were well aware of the dangers they could encounter. They had also promised their families they would return before Christmas. However, days turned into weeks, and one of the climbers started to worry; it seemed increasingly unlikely they would make it back in time. His friend, however, remained hopeful and assured him, "When we reach the next ridge, we will see the path down." When they finally did ascend the ridge, a clear path home indeed lay ahead of them, and they were able to return to their families just in time for the holiday. The friend had provided a glimpse of hope, much like the baby leaping in Elizabeth's womb upon Mary's arrival—a sign that God's promise was near.

Dear brothers and sisters in Christ,

As we gather here today, we immerse ourselves in the Gospel of Luke (1:39-45) a Gospel that speaks volumes about the power of faith, the promise of hope, and the profound interconnectedness of God's children. The meeting between Mary and Elizabeth, two women bound by blood and divine purpose, serves as an epitome of what it means to be vessels of God's grace and conduits of His love.

Elizabeth's baby leaps in her womb as Mary, bearing the Christ child, enters her house. Just as John the Baptist leaps for joy at the closeness of our Savior, so too should our souls be stirred when we encounter the living God in our lives. Elizabeth's joyous exclamation, "Blessed are you among women, and blessed is the fruit of your womb!" is an affirmation we too can experience when we remain open to the movements of the Holy Spirit.

How many times have we been like the uncertain mountaineer, fearful and doubtful of the path ahead? Yet, like the baby leaping in Elizabeth's womb, we too receive signs—sometimes subtle, sometimes monumental—that God's promises are real and unbreakable. In this season of Advent, we are called to be like Mary: courageous, obedient, and willing to journey into the unknown, fortified by faith and the assurance that God is with us.

As we approach the celebration of Christ's birth, let us fortify our faith and be mindful of the little 'leaps' of joy that God places in our path, to confirm that we are, indeed, on the road to fulfilling His divine plan.

Advent is a time of preparation, of quiet contemplation, and of joyful anticipation. Let us be like Mary and Elizabeth, recognizing God's presence in each other and rejoicing in the blessings He bestows upon us. Let this be a season where we truly prepare our hearts to receive the King, making room for Him amidst the busyness and complexities of modern life.

May you find peace, love, and the deep, abiding joy that comes from walking in the ways of the Lord. Amen.

PRAYER:

Gracious and Loving God, as we gather today to commemorate the joyful meeting of Mary and Elizabeth, we are reminded of the unbreakable bonds of faith, love, and divine purpose that You weave into the fabric of our lives. As Elizabeth's child leapt in her womb at the presence of Your Son, may our hearts too be stirred by Your Spirit, filling us with a joy that surpasses all understanding.

In this Advent season, as we await the coming of our Savior, let us be like Mary—courageous in faith, steadfast in hope, and radiant with love. Enable us to recognize Your presence in the faces of those we encounter, and grant us the grace to be vessels of Your peace and goodwill in a world in need.

Lord, we are sometimes burdened by doubt and clouded by uncertainty, much like the mountaineer who questions the path ahead. Yet You, in Your infinite wisdom and compassion, provide us signs and wonders to affirm that Your promises are true. Grant us the grace to perceive these heavenly nudges and the wisdom to interpret them, as we navigate the complexities of our modern lives.

Strengthen our faith, Lord, and deepen our love for You and for one another. Let this time of Advent truly prepare our hearts to receive You, clearing away the distractions and anxieties that can so easily beset us. May we, like Elizabeth and Mary, be united in joyous expectation of the great blessings You are preparing for us.

Through the intercession of St. Elizabeth and the Blessed Virgin Mary, may we come to live in a manner worthy of the call we have received, abiding in Your love, now and forever.

We ask this through Christ, our Lord. Amen.

THE WEEKDAYS OF ADVENT (DECEMBER 22)

READING 1

1 Sm 1:24-28

In those days,
Hannah brought Samuel with her,
along with a three-year-old bull,
an ephah of flour, and a skin of wine,
and presented him at the temple of the LORD in Shiloh.
After the boy's father had sacrificed the young bull,
Hannah, his mother, approached Eli and said:
"Pardon, my lord!
As you live, my lord,
I am the woman who stood near you here, praying to the LORD.
I prayed for this child, and the LORD granted my request.
Now I, in turn, give him to the LORD;
as long as he lives, he shall be dedicated to the LORD."
She left Samuel there.

The word of the Lord.

RESPONSORIAL PSALM

1 Samuel 2:1, 4-5, 6-7, 8abcd

R. (see 1a) My heart exults in the Lord, my Savior.

"My heart exults in the LORD,
my horn is exalted in my God.
I have swallowed up my enemies;
I rejoice in my victory."

R. My heart exults in the Lord, my Savior.

"The bows of the mighty are broken,
while the tottering gird on strength.
The well-fed hire themselves out for bread,
while the hungry batten on spoil.
The barren wife bears seven sons,
while the mother of many languishes."

R. My heart exults in the Lord, my Savior.

"The LORD puts to death and gives life;
he casts down to the nether world;
he raises up again.
The LORD makes poor and makes rich,
he humbles, he also exalts."

R. My heart exults in the Lord, my Savior.

"He raises the needy from the dust;
from the dung heap he lifts up the poor,
To seat them with nobles
and make a glorious throne their heritage."

R. My heart exults in the Lord, my Savior.

ALLELUIA

R. Alleluia, alleluia.
O King of all nations and keystone of the Church:
come and save man, whom you formed from the dust!
R. Alleluia, alleluia.

GOSPEL

Lk 1:46-56

Mary said:

"My soul proclaims the greatness of the Lord;
my spirit rejoices in God my savior.
for he has looked upon his lowly servant.
From this day all generations will call me blessed:
the Almighty has done great things for me,
and holy is his Name.
He has mercy on those who fear him
in every generation.
He has shown the strength of his arm,
and has scattered the proud in their conceit.
He has cast down the mighty from their thrones
and has lifted up the lowly.
He has filled the hungry with good things,
and the rich he has sent away empty.
He has come to the help of his servant Israel
for he remembered his promise of mercy,
the promise he made to our fathers,
to Abraham and his children forever."

Mary remained with Elizabeth about three months
and then returned to her home.

Brothers and sisters, the Gospel of the Lord.

HOMILY:

In the heart of the European Renaissance, an artist named Fra Angelico dedicated himself to depicting Biblical stories through his sacred art. A Dominican friar, he infused his work with deep theological insights. One of his most striking paintings is that of the Visitation, capturing the moment when Mary, pregnant with Jesus, meets her cousin Elizabeth, pregnant with John the Baptist. If one looks closely, the painting seems to be more than just colors and shapes; it vibrates with a silent hymn, a Magnificat, that speaks of the sublime joy and deep spirituality of that sacred meeting. It is as if Fra Angelico has tried to paint not just the event, but the very soul of the Magnificat that Mary proclaims in today's Gospel.

Beloved in Christ, as we draw near to the celebration of our Lord's birth, the Church in her wisdom presents us with the Gospel reading from Luke (1:46-56,) commonly known as the Magnificat. Here, the Blessed Virgin Mary, with a heart full of faith and love, sings her song of praise to God. "My soul magnifies the Lord, and my spirit rejoices in God my Savior." These are not just poetic words but a culmination of deep, theological reflections and the profound mysteries of our faith.

Let us reflect upon three dimensions that the Magnificat opens for us: humility, gratitude, and action.

Humility: Mary acknowledges her lowly state and magnifies the Lord for looking upon her with favor. In a world increasingly focused on self-aggrandizement, where social media often becomes a platform to boast about our achievements, Mary's humility serves as a poignant lesson. St. Augustine, one of the great Doctors of the Church, has often emphasized the importance of humility as the foundation of all other virtues. Like Mary, we too are called to be humble before God, acknowledging that all we have is a gift from Him.

Gratitude: Mary's words exude thanksgiving. She recognizes the great things that God has done for her and rejoices in them. It is easy to forget the blessings we have and focus on what we lack, especially in the fast-paced, often materialistic society we find ourselves in. St. Ignatius of Loyola taught the importance of gratitude in spiritual growth, urging us to take time each day to count our blessings and thank God for them.

Action: The Magnificat is not passive; it tells of a God who actively "has shown strength with his arm; he has scattered the proud in the thoughts of their hearts." God's love is transformative, actively rooting out injustice and sowing the seeds of righteousness and love. St. Teresa of Calcutta embodied this active love, working tirelessly for the "unwanted, unloved, and uncared for."

The Magnificat, dear brothers and sisters, is a mirror into the soul of Mary, but it is also a mirror for us to examine our own lives. As Advent progresses, let this ancient hymn resonate in the sanctuaries of our hearts, motivating us to be humble, grateful, and active in living out our faith.

So let us go forth, imbued with the spirit of Mary's Magnificat, knowing that even in our lowliness and insufficiencies, our souls can magnify the Lord, and our spirits can find eternal joy in God, our Savior. Amen.

PRAYER:

Eternal and Loving Father, as we gather before Your holy presence in this Advent season, we are filled with awe and wonder at the sublime mysteries You have unfolded for our salvation. Today, we meditate upon the Gospel of Luke (1:46-56,) the Magnificat, a divine hymn sung from the depths of the Blessed Virgin Mary's soul, which magnifies Your greatness and mercy.

Lord, just as Mary surrendered herself to Your divine plan with profound humility, enable us to cultivate humble hearts that are receptive to Your word. In a world obsessed with power and status, help us to remember that true greatness lies in submission to Your holy will. May the humility of St. Francis of Assisi, who sought to emulate the simplicity and obedience of Christ, inspire us to walk in similar footsteps.

We offer You thanks, Almighty God, for the uncountable blessings You have showered upon us—blessings that we often take for granted. Kindle within us a spirit of gratitude so that we may acknowledge Your continual love and benevolence. St. Thérèse of Lisieux found You in the simple and mundane; help us to recognize You in the everyday miracles of our lives.

Empower us, O Lord, with a faith that propels us into action. As Mary's Magnificat tells of Your active love for the oppressed, so too may our lives reflect that transformative love in our actions. Inspired by the tireless service of St. Vincent de Paul, grant us the courage to serve the needy, the forgotten, and the marginalized.

May the soul-stirring words of the Magnificat continue to reverberate in our hearts and manifest in our deeds, as we prepare to welcome Your Son, Jesus Christ, into this world and into our lives anew.

We ask all these through Christ, our Lord. Amen.

THE WEEKDAYS OF ADVENT (DECEMBER 23)

READING 1

Mal 3:1-4, 23-24

Thus says the Lord GOD:
Lo, I am sending my messenger
to prepare the way before me;
And suddenly there will come to the temple
the LORD whom you seek,
And the messenger of the covenant whom you desire.
Yes, he is coming, says the LORD of hosts.
But who will endure the day of his coming?
And who can stand when he appears?
For he is like the refiner's fire,
or like the fuller's lye.
He will sit refining and purifying silver,
and he will purify the sons of Levi,
Refining them like gold or like silver
that they may offer due sacrifice to the LORD.
Then the sacrifice of Judah and Jerusalem
will please the LORD,
as in the days of old, as in years gone by.

Lo, I will send you
Elijah, the prophet,
Before the day of the LORD comes,
the great and terrible day,
To turn the hearts of the fathers to their children,
and the hearts of the children to their fathers,
Lest I come and strike
the land with doom.

The word of the Lord.

RESPONSORIAL PSALM

Ps 25:4-5ab, 8-9, 10 and 14

R. (see Luke 21:28) Lift up your heads and see; your redemption is near at hand.

Your ways, O LORD, make known to me;
teach me your paths,
Guide me in your truth and teach me,
for you are God my savior.

R. Lift up your heads and see; your redemption is near at hand.

Good and upright is the LORD;
thus he shows sinners the way.
He guides the humble to justice,
he teaches the humble his way.

R. Lift up your heads and see; your redemption is near at hand.

All the paths of the LORD are kindness and constancy
toward those who keep his covenant and his decrees.
The friendship of the LORD is with those who fear him,
and his covenant, for their instruction.

R. Lift up your heads and see; your redemption is near at hand.

ALLELUIA

R. Alleluia, alleluia.
O King of all nations and keystone of the Church:
come and save man, whom you formed from the dust!
R. Alleluia, alleluia.

GOSPEL

Lk 1:57-66

When the time arrived for Elizabeth to have her child
she gave birth to a son.
Her neighbors and relatives heard
that the Lord had shown his great mercy toward her,
and they rejoiced with her.
When they came on the eighth day to circumcise the child,
they were going to call him Zechariah after his father,
but his mother said in reply,
"No. He will be called John."
But they answered her,
"There is no one among your relatives who has this name."
So they made signs, asking his father what he wished him to be called.
He asked for a tablet and wrote, "John is his name,"
and all were amazed.
Immediately his mouth was opened, his tongue freed,
and he spoke blessing God.
Then fear came upon all their neighbors,
and all these matters were discussed
throughout the hill country of Judea.
All who heard these things took them to heart, saying,
"What, then, will this child be?
For surely the hand of the Lord was with him."

Brothers and sisters, the Gospel of the Lord.

HOMILY:

Consider the story of Thomas Edison, one of the most prominent inventors in history, who once said, "Our greatest weakness lies in giving up. The most certain way to succeed is always to try just one more time." Edison was not just talking about inventing light bulbs or phonographs; he was speaking about the human spirit. Edison faced countless setbacks and failures in his life, but he persisted with resilience and faith. It took him more than 1,000 failed attempts to develop a working light bulb, but he did not lose hope.

Beloved brothers and sisters in Christ, on this day, we are brought closer to the mystery of the Incarnation through the Gospel of Luke (1:57-66.) We hear of the birth of John the Baptist, an event that defied social norms and shattered preconceived notions. Elizabeth and Zechariah, advanced in years and considered barren, become parents to a child who would be the forerunner of the Messiah. This narrative invites us to reflect on the transformative power of God's grace, which can make the seemingly impossible a living reality.

The first lesson is one of faithfulness. Zechariah and Elizabeth, like the Abraham and Sarah of old, remained faithful despite their circumstances. Their faith was tried, but they held fast, much like St. Monica, who prayed tirelessly for the conversion of her son, Augustine. Eventually, their prayers were answered in an extraordinary way. Zechariah, initially struck mute for his doubt, is finally able to speak, and what comes forth is a blessing and a prophecy. His faith has come full circle, and it is now vocal and resolute.

The second lesson is about the importance of names and identities. Zechariah confirms the name "John," which means "God is gracious," as instructed by the angel. In doing so, he affirms the identity and mission of his son. Names are not mere labels; they carry weight and purpose. As baptized Christians, we bear the name of Christ; it is a name that calls us to service, to compassion, and to love. St. Francis de Sales once said, "Have Jesus always for your patron, His Cross for a mast on which you must spread your resolutions as a sail. Your anchor shall be a profound confidence in Him, and you shall sail prosperously."

The final lesson is about the role of community. The birth of John brought joy not only to his parents but also to the neighbors and relatives who recognized the hand of God in these wondrous events. The community plays an indispensable role in acknowledging and affirming the miracles that God performs in our lives.

In community, we help each other make sense of life's complexities, and we find strength in shared faith.

Dear friends, let us embrace the promise of Advent, a season that celebrates the boundless possibilities when humanity cooperates with divine grace. As we await the arrival of our Savior, may we, like Zechariah and Elizabeth, remain steadfast in faith, embrace our Christian identity, and find strength in our community. Amen.

PRAYER:

Heavenly Father, as we gather here in Your divine presence, we find our hearts uplifted by the miraculous birth of John the Baptist, as recounted in the Gospel according to Luke. We are awed by the boundless possibilities that manifest when human limitations are intersected by Your almighty grace. Your wisdom, O God, subverts our expectations, confounds our skepticism, and expands the horizons of our hope.

Lord, we remember Zechariah and Elizabeth, who in their later years, welcomed a child filled with the Holy Spirit. Let their steadfast faith serve as an enduring lesson to us. We ask that You infuse our hearts with a faith that is unyielding in the face of trials, a faith that stands as a beacon in the darkness of doubt. Help us to embrace, just as Zechariah did, the gift of faith that enables us to speak blessings and prophecies to a world in dire need of Your Word.

We are reminded, too, of the meaning carried by names. As Zechariah named his son John, signifying "God is gracious," let us recognize the names we bear as Christians. Let these names serve not as mere labels, but as a call to action— to service, compassion, and love. St. Augustine once said, "To fall in love with God is the greatest romance; to seek Him the greatest adventure; to find Him, the greatest human achievement." May we find our greatest achievement in embodying the love of Christ, whose advent we eagerly await.

In this season of Advent, when Your love took flesh in the Incarnation, we pray for the strength to come together as a community of faith. Through collective prayer and action, let us be the salt of the earth and the light of the world, affirming the miracles You perform in our midst every day.

We offer these petitions in the name of Your Son, Jesus Christ, whose coming we joyfully anticipate. Amen.

THE WEEKDAYS OF ADVENT
(DECEMBER 24)

READING I

2 Sm 7:1-5, 8b-12, 14a, 16

When King David was settled in his palace,
and the LORD had given him rest from his enemies on every side,
he said to Nathan the prophet,
"Here I am living in a house of cedar,
while the ark of God dwells in a tent!"
Nathan answered the king,
"Go, do whatever you have in mind,
for the LORD is with you."
But that night the LORD spoke to Nathan and said:
"Go, tell my servant David, 'Thus says the LORD:
Should you build me a house to dwell in?
"'It was I who took you from the pasture
and from the care of the flock
to be commander of my people Israel.
I have been with you wherever you went,
and I have destroyed all your enemies before you.
And I will make you famous like the great ones of the earth.
I will fix a place for my people Israel;
I will plant them so that they may dwell in their place
without further disturbance.
Neither shall the wicked continue to afflict them as they did of old,
since the time I first appointed judges over my people Israel.
I will give you rest from all your enemies.
The LORD also reveals to you
that he will establish a house for you.
And when your time comes and you rest with your ancestors,
I will raise up your heir after you, sprung from your loins,
and I will make his Kingdom firm.
I will be a father to him,

and he shall be a son to me.
Your house and your Kingdom shall endure forever before me;
your throne shall stand firm forever.'"

The word of the Lord.

RESPONSORIAL PSALM

89:2-3, 4-5, 27 and 29

R. (2) For ever I will sing the goodness of the Lord.

The favors of the LORD I will sing forever;
   through all generations my mouth shall proclaim your faithfulness.
For you have said, "My kindness is established forever";
   in heaven you have confirmed your faithfulness.

R. Forever I will sing the goodness of the Lord.

"I have made a covenant with my chosen one,
   I have sworn to David my servant:
Forever will I confirm your posterity
   and establish your throne for all generations."

R. Forever I will sing the goodness of the Lord.

"He shall say of me, 'You are my father,
   my God, the rock, my savior.'
Forever I will maintain my kindness toward him,
   and my covenant with him stands firm."

R. Forever I will sing the goodness of the Lord.

ALLELUIA

R. Alleluia, alleluia.
O Radiant Dawn,
splendor of eternal light, sun of justice:
come and shine on those who dwell in darkness and in the shadow of death.
R. Alleluia, alleluia.

GOSPEL

Lk 1:67-79

Zechariah his father, filled with the Holy Spirit, prophesied, saying:
"Blessed be the Lord, the God of Israel;
   for he has come to his people and set them free.
He has raised up for us a mighty Savior,
   born of the house of his servant David.
Through his prophets he promised of old
   that he would save us from our enemies,
   from the hands of all who hate us.
He promised to show mercy to our fathers
   and to remember his holy covenant.
This was the oath he swore to our father Abraham:
   to set us free from the hand of our enemies,
   free to worship him without fear,
   holy and righteous in his sight
   all the days of our life.
You, my child, shall be called the prophet of the Most High,
   for you will go before the Lord to prepare his way,
   to give his people knowledge of salvation
   by the forgiveness of their sins.
In the tender compassion of our God
   the dawn from on high shall break upon us,
   to shine on those who dwell in darkness and the shadow of death,
   and to guide our feet into the way of peace."

Brothers and sisters, the Gospel of the Lord.

HOMILY:

The great German theologian Dietrich Bonhoeffer, who stood against Hitler and was eventually martyred for his resistance, once spoke about the "cost of discipleship." He insisted that grace is not cheap; it comes with responsibilities. In the face of grave evil, he lived this belief, willing to make personal sacrifices for the greater good. Much like Zechariah in today's Gospel reading, Bonhoeffer was not simply joyful for the sake of joy, but because he understood the depth of God's plan for mankind—a plan that demanded active participation, personal sacrifice, and unyielding faith.

Beloved in Christ,

As we gather on this eve of the Nativity of our Lord, our hearts are ablaze with the light of anticipation. The Gospel of Luke, in its tender eloquence, portrays Zechariah—filled with the Holy Spirit—as he proclaims a canticle of blessings and promises.

Zechariah's prophetic utterances were not mere expressions of personal joy over the birth of his son, John the Baptist. They were rooted in the historical and eschatological consciousness of Israel. When he said, "Blessed be the Lord God of Israel, for he has visited and brought redemption to his people," he was channeling centuries of hope, sacrifice, and divine promises. The voice of Zechariah resounds as an echo of the voices of Abraham, Isaac, and Jacob; it carries the weight of the covenant that God had established with His people.

Here, dear brothers and sisters, we find a salient lesson. Our joy in this Advent season is not an isolated, individualistic emotion. It is the joy of the Church, the Bride of Christ, as she prepares to welcome the incarnate Word. It is the joy of humanity, as we recognize the universal salvific will of God. As St. Augustine pointedly remarked, "God loves each of us as if there were only one of us." Such is the magnitude of the grace bestowed upon us.

Zechariah teaches us the Christian virtue of hope, a hope that goes beyond mere wishful thinking. It is a theological virtue, deeply rooted in a divine promise. In his words, we hear a poetic depiction of the mission of Jesus, who would come "to shine on those who sit in darkness and in the shadow of death, to guide our feet into the path of peace."

May we, too, be conduits of that divine light. Let us bear in mind the admonition of St. Teresa of Avila, who said, "Christ has no body now but yours. No hands, no feet on earth but yours. Yours are the eyes through which he looks compassion on this world."

As we near the celebration of the Incarnation, may we find the courage to live in accord with the Christian hope illuminated in the words of Zechariah. May we take up the responsibilities that this grace-laden hope places upon us—just as Dietrich Bonhoeffer did, just as countless saints have done—to become active participants in God's redemptive plan for mankind. Amen.

PRAYER:

Most Gracious and Loving Father,

In the quietude of this Advent season, as night gives way to the dawn of Your incarnate Word, we find ourselves humbled in Your divine presence. Assembled in faith, hope, and love, we seek to echo the canticle of Zechariah, exclaiming, "Blessed be the Lord, the God of Israel; he has come to his people and set them free."

Lord, in Your boundless wisdom, You willed the Word to become flesh, bringing the light of salvation into the darkness of our world. As Zechariah proclaimed, Your dawn has truly broken upon us, to shine on those living in the shadow of despair, to guide our feet into the way of peace. We beseech You, let our lives be a living testament to this celestial light, fulfilling Your promise of redemption and liberation.

Enable us, O Father, to internalize the words of Zechariah as not merely a prophecy of times past but as an enduring call to discipleship. Empower us to act justly, to love mercy, and to walk humbly with You, living the theological virtues of faith, hope, and love in a world that often seems bereft of these. Like St. Francis of Assisi, make us instruments of Your peace, sowing love where there is hatred, pardon where there is injury, and unity where there is discord.

As we stand at the cusp of celebrating the miraculous birth of Your Son, Jesus Christ, ignite in our hearts the flame of holy anticipation. As St. Augustine taught us, You love each of us as if there were only one of us. May we, in turn, radiate that love to the world, that all may know the reason for our joy, our peace, and our hope.

In the name of Your Son, our Lord Jesus Christ, who lives and reigns with You and the Holy Spirit, one God, forever and ever. Amen.

CHRISTMAS SEASON (DECEMBER 26)

READING 1

Acts 6:8-10; 7:54-59

Stephen, filled with grace and power,
was working great wonders and signs among the people.
Certain members of the so-called Synagogue of Freedmen,
Cyrenians, and Alexandrians,
and people from Cilicia and Asia,
came forward and debated with Stephen,
but they could not withstand the wisdom and the spirit with which he spoke.

When they heard this, they were infuriated,
and they ground their teeth at him.
But he, filled with the Holy Spirit,
looked up intently to heaven
and saw the glory of God and Jesus standing at the right hand of God,
and he said,
"Behold, I see the heavens opened and the Son of Man
standing at the right hand of God."
But they cried out in a loud voice, covered their ears,
and rushed upon him together.
They threw him out of the city, and began to stone him.
The witnesses laid down their cloaks
at the feet of a young man named Saul.
As they were stoning Stephen, he called out
"Lord Jesus, receive my spirit."

The word of the Lord.

RESPONSORIAL PSALM

Ps 31:3cd-4, 6 and 8ab, 16bc and 17

R. (6) Into your hands, O Lord, I commend my spirit.

Be my rock of refuge,
a stronghold to give me safety.
You are my rock and my fortress;
for your name's sake you will lead and guide me.

R. Into your hands, O Lord, I commend my spirit.

Into your hands I commend my spirit;
you will redeem me, O LORD, O faithful God.
I will rejoice and be glad because of your mercy.

R. Into your hands, O Lord, I commend my spirit.

Rescue me from the clutches of my enemies and my persecutors.
Let your face shine upon your servant;
save me in your kindness.

R. Into your hands, O Lord, I commend my spirit.

ALLELUIA

Ps 118:26a, 27a

R. Alleluia, alleluia.
Blessed is he who comes in the name of the LORD:
the LORD is God and has given us light.
R. Alleluia, alleluia.

GOSPEL

Mt 10:17-22

Jesus said to his disciples:
"Beware of men, for they will hand you over to courts
and scourge you in their synagogues,
and you will be led before governors and kings for my sake
as a witness before them and the pagans.
When they hand you over,
do not worry about how you are to speak
or what you are to say.
You will be given at that moment what you are to say.
For it will not be you who speak
but the Spirit of your Father speaking through you.
Brother will hand over brother to death,
and the father his child;
children will rise up against parents and have them put to death.
You will be hated by all because of my name,
but whoever endures to the end will be saved."

Brothers and sisters, the Gospel of the Lord.

HOMILY:

In the early centuries of Christianity, St. Stephen became the Church's first martyr, his life being a testament to the scripture we reflect upon today. Legend has it that Stephen's demeanor remained calm and Christ-like even as he faced grave persecution. Clothed in the garment of faith and fortified by the Spirit, Stephen saw the heavens opened and Jesus standing at the right hand of God. His last words were a prayer for his persecutors, a mirror to Christ's compassion and mercy. In our times, the courage of St. Stephen serves as a poignant reminder: When adversity surrounds us, we are called not to surrender to despair but to be courageous witnesses of our faith.

Dearly beloved,

On this day following the celebration of Christ's miraculous birth, the Gospel of Matthew presents us with a stark contrast, a solemn reminder of the cost of discipleship. As we gather in the warm embrace of Christmas joy, the Church commemorates the Feast of St. Stephen, the first Christian martyr. Why would the Church position this feast so close to the radiant dawn of Christmas? The answer, dear brethren, lies in the very Gospel we contemplate today.

Jesus cautioned His disciples, saying, "You will be hated by all because of my name, but whoever endures to the end will be saved." In essence, He laid bare the reality that our journey of faith is not a promenade in a rose garden; it demands sacrifice, endurance, and oftentimes, suffering. St. Augustine once said, "God had one son on earth without sin, but never one without suffering." Hence, even as the fragrance of frankincense still lingers in the air, the Church wisely nudges us to remember the cost of our fidelity to Christ.

In the panorama of Christian history, countless men and women have borne the weight of the cross, finding their inspiration in Christ and His early disciples. St. Stephen, whose feast we celebrate today, was imbued with such divine wisdom and grace that even the prospect of stoning did not deter him from witnessing to the truth. Just like his Lord, Stephen prayed for his persecutors, encapsulating the essence of Christian forgiveness and courage.

In our modern world, we may not face persecution in the same way that the early Christians did. Yet, every insult we endure, every sacrifice we make for the sake of righteousness, every ethical dilemma we navigate while upholding our moral and religious principles—these are the stones of our time. And in these moments, we are invited to emulate St. Stephen, looking heavenward and finding the strength to remain steadfast in our faith.

In the Liturgy of the Eucharist, as the bread and wine are lifted up, let us also elevate our hearts and minds to the Almighty. Let us pray for the courage to live our faith boldly and authentically, even in the face of adversity. As we continue to traverse the luminous season of Christmas, may we not forget the shadows that deepen the contrast, allowing the light of Christ to shine ever brighter in our lives. Amen.

PRAYER:

Heavenly Father, who is both the Alpha and the Omega, the birth and rebirth of all things good,

On this day, as the world is still aglow with the celestial light of the Nativity, we come before You with hearts rejoicing yet minds pondering. For today, the Church commemorates the Feast of St. Stephen, Your valiant martyr, who, with unwavering faith, stood as a beacon of Your unending love and grace.

In the Gospel of Matthew, Your Son, Jesus Christ, warns us that to follow Him may mean to tread a path of difficulty and persecution. "You will be hated by all because of my name," He says, reminding us that the call to discipleship is a call to courageous fidelity in face of opposition. As we revel in the joys of this Christmas season, let us not forget the cost of the salvation we so freely celebrate. May we, inspired by the fortitude of St. Stephen, find courage to bear our own crosses, however they may manifest in our lives.

We pray for the Church, that it may be a sanctuary of hope and a fortress of faith for all who are persecuted for Your Name's sake. We pray for our world, that the peace heralded by the birth of the Prince of Peace may penetrate even the darkest corners of human suffering and injustice.

Strengthen us, O Lord, in our daily trials and tribulations, that we may never falter in our mission to live and share the Gospel. Infuse us with the same Spirit that led St. Stephen to look toward Heaven in his final moments, so that we too may catch a glimpse of Your glory even amidst our earthly struggles.

May our lives be a ceaseless hymn of praise to You, echoing the songs of the angels that announced the birth of our Savior, Christ the Lord. Through the same Christ our Lord, who lives and reigns with You and the unity of the Holy Spirit, one God, forever and ever. Amen.

CHRISTMAS SEASON (DECEMBER 27)

READING 1

1 Jn 1:1-4

Beloved:
What was from the beginning,
what we have heard,
what we have seen with our eyes,
what we looked upon
and touched with our hands
concerns the Word of life —
for the life was made visible;
we have seen it and testify to it
and proclaim to you the eternal life
that was with the Father and was made visible to us—
what we have seen and heard
we proclaim now to you,
so that you too may have fellowship with us;
for our fellowship is with the Father
and with his Son, Jesus Christ.
We are writing this so that our joy may be complete.

The word of the Lord.

RESPONSORIAL PSALM

Ps 97:1-2, 5-6, 11-12

R. (12) Rejoice in the Lord, you just!
The LORD is king; let the earth rejoice;
let the many isles be glad.
Clouds and darkness are around him,
justice and judgment are the foundation of his throne.

R. Rejoice in the Lord, you just!

The mountains melt like wax before the LORD,
before the LORD of all the earth.
The heavens proclaim his justice,
and all peoples see his glory.

R. Rejoice in the Lord, you just!

Light dawns for the just;
and gladness, for the upright of heart.
Be glad in the LORD, you just,
and give thanks to his holy name.

R. Rejoice in the Lord, you just!

ALLELUIA SEE

R. Alleluia, alleluia.
We praise you, O God,
we acclaim you as Lord;
the glorious company of Apostles praise you.
R. Alleluia, alleluia.

GOSPEL

Jn 20:1a and 2-8

On the first day of the week,
Mary Magdalene ran and went to Simon Peter
and to the other disciple whom Jesus loved, and told them,
"They have taken the Lord from the tomb,
and we do not know where they put him."
So Peter and the other disciple went out and came to the tomb.
They both ran, but the other disciple ran faster than Peter
and arrived at the tomb first;
he bent down and saw the burial cloths there, but did not go in.
When Simon Peter arrived after him,
he went into the tomb and saw the burial cloths there,
and the cloth that had covered his head,
not with the burial cloths but rolled up in a separate place.
Then the other disciple also went in,
the one who had arrived at the tomb first,
and he saw and believed.

Brothers and sisters, the Gospel of the Lord.

HOMILY:

In a humble monastery long ago, the monks maintained an extraordinary practice during Christmas. They would bring a mirror and place it next to the Nativity scene set up in the chapel. The mirror stood there not for vanity but for reflection—literally and metaphorically. It was placed at such an angle that whoever looked into it would see themselves alongside the Holy Family, the Wise Men, and the shepherds. The message was clear: You are part of this story. You are a witness to these miracles. The elder monk would often say, "To truly understand the Nativity, you must see yourself as a part of it, not separate, for every Christmas is a call to recognize the ongoing incarnation of God's love in our lives."

Dear brothers and sisters in Christ,

On this third day in the Octave of Christmas, we find ourselves in a somewhat enigmatic Gospel reading from John, which may appear initially disconnected from the Nativity narrative. The Gospel describes how St. John the Apostle and St. Peter discovered the empty tomb of Jesus on Easter morning. You may wonder: What does Easter have to do with Christmas?

Ah, but here lies a divine juxtaposition that takes us to the very essence of our Christian journey. We are reminded today that the joy of Christ's birth leads us to the ultimate joy of His resurrection. The Gospel invites us to consider the entirety of Christ's life, His birth, death, and resurrection, as one inseparable reality. Just as St. John the Apostle was a witness to both the beginning and the completion of Christ's earthly mission, so too are we called to be vigilant witnesses to God's work in the world.

By looking into the metaphorical mirror next to the Nativity, we can understand that the birth of Christ is not just an event that happened more than two thousand years ago; it is a reality that needs to be lived, experienced, and testified to, just like the empty tomb. St. Augustine once said, "We are an Easter people and 'Alleluia' is our song!" But let us also remember that before Easter, we were a Christmas people, and our song was "Gloria in Excelsis Deo!"

In this Christmas season, and throughout our lives, may we ever be conscious of the miracles we are called to witness: both the miracle of the God who came as a vulnerable baby and the miracle of the empty tomb that proclaims death is not the end. May we heed the call to be witnesses—true disciples who not only look but also see, not only hear but also listen, and not only exist but also live in the luminous reality of God's everlasting love.

Let us continue to place ourselves in the ongoing story of God's magnificent plan for salvation, being ever mindful that the crib and the cross are made of the same wood: the wood of humanity's hope, salvation, and redemption. Amen.

PRAYER:

Almighty and Eternal God, as we gather in the stillness of this blessed Christmas season, our hearts brimming with awe and gratitude, we find ourselves juxtaposed with the paradox of the Gospel today—of a tomb emptied and linens left behind. We stand here contemplating the mystery of Your Son's birth even as we are reminded of His glorious resurrection.

Lord, as the Gospel of John nudges us toward Easter, fortify in us the understanding that Christmas is but the first chapter in the salvific narrative You have written for humanity. As St. John the Apostle was a witness to both Your incarnation and Your resurrection, may we too witness Your enduring presence in our lives, in joys and sorrows, in simplicity and complexity, in the crib and at the cross.

Illuminate us this day to grasp the continuum of Your divine love, which began in Bethlehem and found its fullness in the empty tomb. As St. John the Apostle was graced with the wisdom to see and believe, grant us the same grace, Lord. May our faith not be a fragmented collection of doctrines, but a unified tapestry that merges the joys of Your birth and the hope of Your resurrection.

During this Octave of Christmas, may our hearts remain open to the beauty of Your wondrous deeds. May we never cease to be a Christmas people in a world that so deeply needs the peace, the hope, and the love that both the Nativity and the Resurrection offer. Help us to be your hands and feet, witnessing to Your eternal love and boundless mercy in every season of our lives.

In the name of Your Son, Jesus Christ, born of the Virgin Mary, crucified, and risen for our salvation, we offer this prayer. Amen.

CHRISTMAS SEASON (DECEMBER 28) FEAST OF THE HOLY INNOCENTS, MARTYRS

READING 1

1 Jn 1:5—2:2

Beloved:
This is the message that we have heard from Jesus Christ
and proclaim to you:
God is light, and in him there is no darkness at all.
If we say, "We have fellowship with him,"
while we continue to walk in darkness,
we lie and do not act in truth.
But if we walk in the light as he is in the light,
then we have fellowship with one another,
and the Blood of his Son Jesus cleanses us from all sin.
If we say, "We are without sin,"
we deceive ourselves, and the truth is not in us.
If we acknowledge our sins, he is faithful and just
and will forgive our sins and cleanse us from every wrongdoing.
If we say, "We have not sinned," we make him a liar,
and his word is not in us.

My children, I am writing this to you
so that you may not commit sin.
But if anyone does sin, we have an Advocate with the Father,
Jesus Christ the righteous one.
He is expiation for our sins,
and not for our sins only but for those of the whole world.

The word of the Lord.

RESPONSORIAL PSALM

Ps 124:2-3, 4-5, 7cd-8

R. (7) Our soul has been rescued like a bird from the fowler's snare.

Had not the LORD been with us—
When men rose up against us,
then would they have swallowed us alive,
When their fury was inflamed against us.

R. Our soul has been rescued like a bird from the fowler's snare.

Then would the waters have overwhelmed us;
The torrent would have swept over us;
over us then would have swept the raging waters.

R. Our soul has been rescued like a bird from the fowler's snare.

Broken was the snare,
and we were freed.
Our help is in the name of the LORD,
who made heaven and earth.

R. Our soul has been rescued like a bird from the fowler's snare.

ALLELUIA SEE

R. Alleluia, alleluia.
We praise you, O God,
we acclaim you as Lord;
the white robed army of martyrs praise you.
R. Alleluia, alleluia.

GOSPEL

Mt 2:13-18

When the magi had departed, behold,
the angel of the Lord appeared to Joseph in a dream and said,
"Rise, take the child and his mother, flee to Egypt,
and stay there until I tell you.
Herod is going to search for the child to destroy him."
Joseph rose and took the child and his mother by night
and departed for Egypt.
He stayed there until the death of Herod,
that what the Lord had said through the prophet might be fulfilled,
Out of Egypt I called my son.

When Herod realized that he had been deceived by the magi,
he became furious.
He ordered the massacre of all the boys in Bethlehem and its vicinity
two years old and under,
in accordance with the time he had ascertained from the magi.
Then was fulfilled what had been said through Jeremiah the prophet:

A voice was heard in Ramah,
sobbing and loud lamentation;
Rachel weeping for her children,
and she would not be consoled,
since they were no more.

Brothers and sisters, the Gospel of the Lord.

HOMILY:

In the ancient city of Coventry, England, stands a cathedral that tells a poignant tale of loss and renewal. During World War II, the cathedral was bombed and almost entirely destroyed. Yet, from its ruins grew a resolve to seek reconciliation rather than revenge. A cross made from charred beams and a humble inscription, "Father Forgive," mark the site today. Much like the tale of the Holy Innocents, this cathedral stands as a testament to the mystery of God bringing good out of evil, life out of death.

My dear brothers and sisters in Christ,

On this solemn Feast of the Holy Innocents, we are confronted with a stark and unsettling Gospel—a narrative that seems far removed from the joy and celebration of the Christmas season we are in. Yet, paradoxically, it is deeply entwined with the very purpose of Christ's coming into the world.

Today's Gospel recounts the brutal episode of King Herod's massacre of innocent children in an attempt to kill the infant Jesus. Herod, drowning in his own insecurity and paranoia, orchestrates an atrocity that echoes through the corridors of time. However, let us remember what St. Augustine so wisely noted: "The death of the Holy Innocents bears witness to the fact that man's salvation is accomplished not by man, but through God."

In our modern world, where the sanctity of life is increasingly undermined, the Feast of the Holy Innocents serves as a crucial ethical and theological anchor. It is a solemn reminder that the promise of Christmas, the gift of the Incarnation, is the restoration of dignity to the lowly, voice to the voiceless, and life to those who suffer under the yoke of death.

The innocence of the children who lost their lives is a mirror, reflecting the innocence and purity of Christ Himself, who would later be sacrificed for the redemption of humanity. Their lives were not in vain; they are martyrs, baptized by a baptism of blood, as early Christian tradition tells us. And so, we find in their tragic death a strange, divine irony: in attempting to kill the Source of Life, Herod raises up the first martyrs for Christ, the very children who precede Christ into Heaven.

As we remember the Holy Innocents today, let us not shy away from the challenging questions and uncomfortable feelings this feast evokes. How do we stand up for the innocent and voiceless today? How do we protect life in all its stages? The call to each of us is to make our own lives, in whatever way possible, a witness to the dignity and sanctity of human life—from conception to natural death.

In this Eucharistic celebration, let us remember that the same Jesus who escaped the sword of Herod would one day willingly lay down His life for our salvation. In so doing, He conquered death forever, validating the hope and the tears of all innocents who have suffered throughout the ages.

May the Holy Innocents intercede for us, and may we be fortified by their example to live as advocates for all those innocents who today are endangered by the Herods of our time. Amen.

PRAYER:

O Almighty and Everlasting God, who in Your wisdom and love ordered the universe and set the days and seasons in their courses, we come before You on this Feast of the Holy Innocents.

We are struck, Lord, by the contrast between the innocence of the child in Bethlehem and the cruel decree of Herod. In a world that too often preys upon the innocent, we are called to remember these little martyrs, who have gone before us in bearing witness to Your gift of life. May their purity and your grace inspire us to defend the voiceless and the vulnerable among us.

Lord Jesus, You came as the Prince of Peace, and yet Your presence ignited a fury that resulted in profound suffering. Teach us to understand that the peace you bring is not without cost, that it demands of us courage and fortitude to stand against the powers of evil and darkness.

We ask, O Lord, for the strength to be ever vigilant in protecting the sanctity of life, from conception to natural death. Fortify our resolve to be advocates for justice, stewards of mercy, and instruments of Your peace in this troubled world.

May the Holy Innocents, who were privileged to be numbered among the earliest of Your martyrs, intercede on behalf of all innocents who suffer today—whether by poverty, by war, by illness, or any form of injustice. May their cries reach Your heavenly throne and awaken in us a renewed commitment to act justly, love tenderly, and walk humbly with You, our God.

Through Christ, our Lord, who lives and reigns with You and the unity of the Holy Spirit, One God, forever and ever. Amen.

CHRISTMAS SEASON (DECEMBER 29) THE FIFTH DAY IN THE OCTAVE OF CHRISTMAS

READING 1

1 Jn 2:3-11

Beloved:
The way we may be sure that we know Jesus
is to keep his commandments.
Whoever says, "I know him," but does not keep his commandments
is a liar, and the truth is not in him.
But whoever keeps his word,
the love of God is truly perfected in him.
This is the way we may know that we are in union with him:
whoever claims to abide in him ought to walk just as he walked.

Beloved, I am writing no new commandment to you
but an old commandment that you had from the beginning.
The old commandment is the word that you have heard.
And yet I do write a new commandment to you,
which holds true in him and among you,
for the darkness is passing away,
and the true light is already shining.
Whoever says he is in the light,
yet hates his brother, is still in the darkness.
Whoever loves his brother remains in the light,
and there is nothing in him to cause a fall.
Whoever hates his brother is in darkness;
he walks in darkness and does not know where he is going
because the darkness has blinded his eyes.
The word of the Lord.

RESPONSORIAL PSALM

Ps 96:1-2a, 2b-3, 5b-6

R. (11a) Let the heavens be glad and the earth rejoice!

Sing to the LORD a new song;
sing to the LORD, all you lands.
Sing to the LORD; bless his name.

R. Let the heavens be glad and the earth rejoice!

Announce his salvation, day after day.
Tell his glory among the nations;
among all peoples, his wondrous deeds.

R. Let the heavens be glad and the earth rejoice!

The LORD made the heavens.
Splendor and majesty go before him;
praise and grandeur are in his sanctuary.

R. Let the heavens be glad and the earth rejoice!

ALLELUIA

Lk 2:32

R. Alleluia, alleluia.
A light of revelation to the Gentiles
and glory for your people Israel.
R. Alleluia, alleluia.

GOSPEL

Lk 2:22-35

When the days were completed for their purification
according to the law of Moses,
the parents of Jesus took him up to Jerusalem
to present him to the Lord,
just as it is written in the law of the Lord,
Every male that opens the womb shall be consecrated to the Lord,
and to offer the sacrifice of
a pair of turtledoves or two young pigeons,
in accordance with the dictate in the law of the Lord.

Now there was a man in Jerusalem whose name was Simeon.
This man was righteous and devout,
awaiting the consolation of Israel,
and the Holy Spirit was upon him.
It had been revealed to him by the Holy Spirit
that he should not see death
before he had seen the Christ of the Lord.
He came in the Spirit into the temple;
and when the parents brought in the child Jesus
to perform the custom of the law in regard to him,
he took him into his arms and blessed God, saying:

"Lord, now let your servant go in peace;
your word has been fulfilled:
my own eyes have seen the salvation
which you prepared in the sight of every people,
a light to reveal you to the nations
and the glory of your people Israel."

The child's father and mother were amazed at what was said about him;
and Simeon blessed them and said to Mary his mother,
"Behold, this child is destined
for the fall and rise of many in Israel,
and to be a sign that will be contradicted
(and you yourself a sword will pierce)
so that the thoughts of many hearts may be revealed."

Brothers and sisters, the Gospel of the Lord.

HOMILY:

The story is told of a skilled violinist who crafted an exquisite piece on his violin, putting his soul into every note. When he finished, he left the violin on a table and stepped away. Someone else picked up the violin and tried to play it but only produced discordant sounds. The violin was the same, but the hands were different. The lesson here is that the same instrument can bring forth drastically different outcomes depending on who handles it.

My dear brothers and sisters, as we gather on this Fifth Day in the Octave of Christmas, the Gospel of Luke presents us with the story of the Presentation of the Lord in the Temple. In the narrative, Simeon, a devout man awaiting the consolation of Israel, recognizes the infant Jesus as the promised Messiah and speaks profound words: "Now, Master, you may let your servant go in peace, according to your word, for my eyes have seen your salvation."

Just like the violin in our story, the child Jesus is an "instrument" in the hands of God, destined to bring forth beautiful "music"—the message of salvation. But it is critical who "plays" this instrument, who interprets its meaning. Simeon understands the promise and potential encapsulated in this child. Yet, he also speaks of a "sign that will be contradicted," hinting at the discordant sounds that the world will produce when trying to understand Jesus.

Simeon's life is changed because he sees in Jesus the fulfillment of God's promise. He understands that this child will be a "light for revelation to the Gentiles, and glory for your people Israel." Simeon's wisdom teaches us that true insight doesn't come merely from human logic but from an openness to the promptings of the Holy Spirit.

But let us not forget the sobering prophecy Simeon addresses to Mary: "And you yourself a sword will pierce." Mary, the Mother of God, will have her heart broken by the very life she nurtured, a poignant reminder that love and suffering often go hand in hand. This warns us that our commitment to Christ, while it may bring joy and fulfillment, will also bring trials and sacrifices. The instrument of God's love, when taken up by human hands, can sometimes produce discord—misunderstanding, persecution, and even death.

In these days of celebration, let us strive to be like Simeon, recognizing and receiving the Christ Child for who He truly is—the Savior of the world. Let's endeavor to be the skilled violinists who bring forth the beautiful music intended by the Creator.

And let us remember that even when our melody is met with discord from the world, we are called to play on, faithfully and courageously, until our own eyes have seen the salvation prepared in the presence of all peoples.

In this way, we can truly live out the essence of this Christmas season, bearing witness to the light that no darkness can overcome. Amen.

PRAYER:

Heavenly Father, Creator of all that is seen and unseen, we gather before You in a spirit of humble adoration, especially as we celebrate the Fifth Day in the Octave of Christmas. On this day, we reflect upon the Gospel of Luke, where Simeon, filled with the Holy Spirit, recognized the Infant Jesus as the light of revelation and the glory of Israel.

Oh Lord, grant us the grace of spiritual discernment to recognize You in the various seasons of our lives. Just as Simeon waited faithfully for the promise of Your salvation, may we too wait with hopeful hearts, attuned to the guidance of the Holy Spirit. Fill us with wisdom to discern the divine in the ordinary, and the eternal in the temporal.

We are especially mindful of Mary, our Blessed Mother, who heard Simeon's prophetic words of joy, but also of sorrow. Grant us the strength, O God, to stand firm in faith even when we, like Mary, are pierced by swords of sorrow or misunderstanding. Let our lives be so anchored in Your love that we can endure the trials of this world with unwavering faith.

We also lift up those among us who are awaiting consolation, those weighed down by life's burdens or struggling in darkness. May the example of Simeon bring hope, and the light of Christ shine upon them, illuminating their paths and warming their hearts.

We ask this in the name of Jesus, the Light of the World and the Glory of Your people, who lives and reigns with You and the Holy Spirit, one God, forever and ever. Amen.

CHRISTMAS SEASON (DECEMBER 30) THE SIXTH DAY IN THE OCTAVE OF CHRISTMAS

READING 1

1 Jn 2:12-17

I am writing to you, children,
because your sins have been forgiven for his name's sake.

I am writing to you, fathers,
because you know him who is from the beginning.

I am writing to you, young men,
because you have conquered the Evil One.

I write to you, children,
because you know the Father.

I write to you, fathers,
because you know him who is from the beginning.

I write to you, young men,
because you are strong and the word of God remains in you,
and you have conquered the Evil One.

Do not love the world or the things of the world.
If anyone loves the world, the love of the Father is not in him.
For all that is in the world,
sensual lust, enticement for the eyes, and a pretentious life,
is not from the Father but is from the world.
Yet the world and its enticement are passing away.

But whoever does the will of God remains forever.
The word of the Lord.

RESPONSIORIAL PSALM

Ps 96:7-8a, 8b-9, 10

R. (11a) Let the heavens be glad and the earth rejoice!

Give to the LORD, you families of nations,
give to the LORD glory and praise;
give to the LORD the glory due his name!

R. Let the heavens be glad and the earth rejoice!

Bring gifts, and enter his courts;
worship the LORD in holy attire.
Tremble before him, all the earth.

R. Let the heavens be glad and the earth rejoice!

Say among the nations: The LORD is king.
He has made the world firm, not to be moved;
he governs the peoples with equity.

R. Let the heavens be glad and the earth rejoice!

ALLELUIA

R. Alleluia, alleluia.
A holy day has dawned upon us.
Come, you nations, and adore the Lord.
Today a great light has come upon the earth.
R. Alleluia, alleluia.

GOSPEL

Lk 2:36-40

There was a prophetess, Anna,
the daughter of Phanuel, of the tribe of Asher.
She was advanced in years,
having lived seven years with her husband after her marriage,
and then as a widow until she was eighty-four.
She never left the temple,
but worshiped night and day with fasting and prayer.
And coming forward at that very time,
she gave thanks to God and spoke about the child
to all who were awaiting the redemption of Jerusalem.

When they had fulfilled all the prescriptions
of the law of the Lord,
they returned to Galilee,
to their own town of Nazareth.
The child grew and became strong, filled with wisdom;
and the favor of God was upon him.

Brothers and sisters, the Gospel of the Lord.

HOMILY:

In the 13th century, St. Thomas Aquinas found himself in conversation with Brother John, who humbly wondered how one could ever truly know God. St. Thomas, who had written extensive theological works, simply pointed to the cross and then to the celebration of the Eucharist. He emphasized that wisdom was not just intellectual knowledge, but a lived experience, a continuity of the mind and heart. Much like Anna the Prophetess in today's Gospel, he spent his years, not just studying and teaching, but also in intimate prayer and fasting.

Dear brothers and sisters in Christ, as we gather on this Sixth Day in the Octave of Christmas, we find ourselves in contemplation of the Gospel of Luke, where the Prophetess Anna is introduced. Anna, an elderly widow, dedicates her life to the service of God, fasting and praying in the Temple day and night. In her, we see the virtues of patience, faithfulness, and spiritual wisdom—a wisdom that can only come from a lived relationship with God.

Her tale is one of quiet heroism, a life lived in the margins yet wholly dedicated to God. Like St. Thomas Aquinas and countless others throughout the annals of faith, Anna knows that intellectual knowledge alone is not enough to truly understand and experience God. Her wisdom is the fruit of a lifetime of prayer and spiritual intimacy, a silent and ongoing dialogue with her Creator.

Anna is a beacon of light, illuminating the way for us in our modern world that so often forgets the value of stillness, of contemplation, and of a life dedicated to spiritual things. She teaches us that wisdom is not the sole domain of scholars and theologians, but is accessible to anyone who opens their heart to God's guidance.

She also shows us that our role in the Kingdom of God does not expire with age or societal standing. She could have easily succumbed to despair, living as a widow, often seen as marginalized in her time. Yet she becomes a prophetess, a title of great spiritual weight. Her joy upon seeing the infant Jesus and recognizing Him as the redeemer is not just personal but shared—she speaks "about the child to all who were looking forward to the redemption of Jerusalem."

So, as we continue this Christmas season, let us strive to emulate Anna. Whether we are in the bloom of youth or in the winter of our years, whether we are well-versed in theological debate or simple in our understanding, let us dedicate ourselves to the pursuit of wisdom through a lived relationship with God. Let us remember that it is never too late, nor are we ever too insignificant, to play a meaningful role in the unfolding of God's redemptive plan.

In this way, our lives will not merely be inscriptions in the sand, easily washed away, but etched in the eternal book of life, illuminated by the everlasting light of Christ. Amen.

PRAYER:

Gracious and Eternal Father, as we gather on this sixth day within the Octave of Christmas, we are humbled and inspired by the example of the Prophetess Anna, as revealed to us in the Gospel of Luke. Through her life of steadfast prayer and fasting, she found the wisdom and grace to recognize the Child Jesus as the long-awaited Messiah.

Lord, we beseech You to imbue us with the same unwavering dedication to spiritual matters, despite the distractions and enticements of our modern world. Just as Anna never ceased to serve You in the temple, may we make our lives a living temple where You reside. Guide us, O Lord, to be vigilant and patient, always seeking and awaiting Your presence in our lives.

As Anna spread the news of Jesus' coming to all who were awaiting redemption, give us the courage to be messengers of Your Good News. Let us be quick to share our joy and hope with those in despair, the peace of Christ with those in conflict, and Your unending love with those who feel abandoned or marginalized.

May we always remember that our years on Earth are not an epilogue but a prologue, a preface to an everlasting communion with You. May our actions and thoughts be directed towards serving You and fulfilling Your divine plan, just as Your servant Anna did, until her life's very twilight.

Through the intercession of the Blessed Virgin Mary, Mother of God, and all the saints who have gone before us, may we walk in the footsteps of Anna—faithful, vigilant, and eternally devoted to You. We ask this in the name of Your Son, Jesus Christ, the Light of the World, who lives and reigns with You and the Holy Spirit, one God forever and ever. Amen.

CHRISTMAS SEASON (DECEMBER 31) THE SEVENTH DAY IN THE OCTAVE OF CHRISTMAS

READING I

1 Jn 2:18-21

Children, it is the last hour;
and just as you heard that the antichrist was coming,
so now many antichrists have appeared.
Thus we know this is the last hour.
They went out from us, but they were not really of our number;
if they had been, they would have remained with us.
Their desertion shows that none of them was of our number.
But you have the anointing that comes from the Holy One,
and you all have knowledge.
I write to you not because you do not know the truth
but because you do, and because every lie is alien to the truth.

The word of the Lord.

RESPONSORIAL PSALM

96:1-2, 11-12, 13

R. (11a) Let the heavens be glad and the earth rejoice!

Sing to the LORD a new song;
  sing to the LORD, all you lands.
Sing to the LORD; bless his name;
  announce his salvation, day after day.

R. Let the heavens be glad and the earth rejoice!

Let the heavens be glad and the earth rejoice;
  let the sea and what fills it resound;
  let the plains be joyful and all that is in them!
Then shall all the trees of the forest exult before the LORD.

R. Let the heavens be glad and the earth rejoice!

The LORD comes,
  he comes to rule the earth.
He shall rule the world with justice
  and the peoples with his constancy.

R. Let the heavens be glad and the earth rejoice!

ALLELUIA

Jn 1:14a, 12a

R. Alleluia, alleluia.
The Word of God became flesh and dwelt among us.
To those who accepted him
he gave power to become the children of God.
R. Alleluia, alleluia.

GOSPEL

Jn 1:1-18

In the beginning was the Word,
   and the Word was with God,
   and the Word was God.
He was in the beginning with God.
All things came to be through him,
   and without him nothing came to be.
What came to be through him was life,
   and this life was the light of the human race;
   the light shines in the darkness,
   and the darkness has not overcome it.
A man named John was sent from God.
He came for testimony, to testify to the light,
so that all might believe through him.
He was not the light,
but came to testify to the light.
The true light, which enlightens everyone, was coming into the world.
He was in the world,
   and the world came to be through him,
   but the world did not know him.
He came to what was his own,
   but his own people did not accept him.
But to those who did accept him
   he gave power to become children of God,
   to those who believe in his name,
   who were born not by natural generation
   nor by human choice nor by a man's decision
   but of God.
And the Word became flesh
   and made his dwelling among us,
   and we saw his glory,
   the glory as of the Father's only-begotten Son,
   full of grace and truth.
John testified to him and cried out, saying,
"This was he of whom I said,
'The one who is coming after me ranks ahead of me
because he existed before me.'"
From his fullness we have all received,
grace in place of grace,

because while the law was given through Moses,
grace and truth came through Jesus Christ.
No one has ever seen God.
The only-begotten Son, God, who is at the Father's side,
has revealed him.

Brothers and sisters, the Gospel of the Lord.

HOMILY:

The world-renowned physicist Albert Einstein was once asked by a young student, "Professor, do you believe in God?" Einstein replied, "I believe in the God of Spinoza." Baruch Spinoza, a 17th-century philosopher, had a view of God as a singular, infinite substance that constitutes the universe itself. His thoughts reflect the notion of a God who is inseparable from all of creation, yet not a personal God who answers prayers. Einstein's perspective, like that of Spinoza, echoes the theological profundity we encounter in today's Gospel of John (1:1-18) where we are reminded that God is both immanent and transcendent, a God who is both the Word and the Light that enlightens every human being.

Dear brothers and sisters in Christ,

As we come to the close of the year, we gather on this seventh day within the Octave of Christmas to contemplate the profound mystery expressed in today's Gospel from John: "In the beginning was the Word, and the Word was with God, and the Word was God." These opening lines are not just poetic; they invite us to dive into the depths of God's eternal nature and His intimate relationship with humanity.

The Gospel of John teaches us that the Word became flesh. This is an astonishing claim that sets Christianity apart. God did not just send a messenger, an angel, or a set of laws; God Himself entered into the fabric of our existence. As St. Augustine observed, "God became man so that man might become God." The Incarnation is an expression of God's unconditional love and a call to elevate our human nature.

In the cultural milieu of our modern world, we find the commercialization of faith, the aggrandizement of material wealth, and the erosion of moral and spiritual values. Yet, the Word made flesh is a light that shines in the darkness, and the darkness has not overcome it. The Gospel reminds us that true light and wisdom come from an encounter with Jesus Christ, the Word made flesh.

Let us be like John the Baptist, who was not the light but came to testify to the light. We are called to be witnesses, to testify to this eternal light in a world darkened by moral relativism and spiritual emptiness. It's not an easy task, but it's a fulfilling one. As Thomas Merton, the Trappist monk and mystic, once said, "To be a saint means to be myself. Therefore, the problem of sanctity and salvation is, in fact, the problem of finding out who I am and of discovering my true self."

So as the year comes to a close, let us not just make resolutions that benefit our physical or emotional selves but also those that edify our spiritual lives. For in understanding the Word, we come to understand God; and in understanding God, we come to understand ourselves.

Let us move into the new year as people enlightened by the Word, embodying the compassion, justice, and love that Jesus Christ brought into the world, for by doing so, we allow others to see the radiant face of God. Amen.

PRAYER:

Eternal and Most Gracious God,

We come before You on this next to last day of the year, standing at the intersection of time past and time yet to unfold. We gather as Your people, illuminated by the Light of the World, our Lord and Savior, Jesus Christ, as revealed in today's Gospel of John.

Father, we meditate on the profound mystery that "In the beginning was the Word, and the Word was with God, and the Word was God." As we close another chapter in our earthly sojourn, we pause to contemplate the immeasurable love that led You to become one like us, the Word made flesh dwelling among us. For this wondrous act, we offer You ceaseless praise and everlasting gratitude.

As the Gospel recounts that Your light shines in the darkness and the darkness has not overcome it, we earnestly beseech You to illumine our hearts and minds with this Eternal Light. Dispel any shadow of doubt, confusion, or despair that clouds our vision and journey.

Let us be, like John the Baptist, faithful witnesses to the Light, heralding Your boundless mercy, justice, and love in a world that so desperately needs them. Bless our efforts to manifest Your Kingdom here on Earth, that we might walk in the true path illuminated by the Gospel truths.

As we stand at the threshold of a new year, we beseech Your blessings of wisdom, courage, and discernment. Grant that we may resolutely turn the pages of this next chapter in alignment with Your Divine Will, anchored in the abiding presence of the Word incarnate, Christ our Lord.

We offer this prayer in the name of Jesus, the Light of the World, who lives and reigns with You and the unity of the Holy Spirit, One God, forever and ever. Amen.

WEEKDAYS OF CHRISTMAS TIME FROM JANUARY 2 TO THE EPIPHANY OF THE LORD

READING 1

1 JN 2:22-28

Beloved:
Who is the liar?
Whoever denies that Jesus is the Christ.
Whoever denies the Father and the Son, this is the antichrist.
Anyone who denies the Son does not have the Father,
but whoever confesses the Son has the Father as well.
Let what you heard from the beginning remain in you.
If what you heard from the beginning remains in you,
then you will remain in the Son and in the Father.
And this is the promise that he made us: eternal life.
I write you these things about those who would deceive you.
As for you,
the anointing that you received from him remains in you,
so that you do not need anyone to teach you.
But his anointing teaches you about everything and is true and not false;
just as it taught you, remain in him.

And now, children, remain in him,
so that when he appears we may have confidence
and not be put to shame by him at his coming.

The word of the Lord.

RESPONSORIAL PSALM

98:1, 2-3AB, 3CD-4

R. (3cd) All the ends of the earth have seen the saving power of God.

Sing to the LORD a new song,
for he has done wondrous deeds;
His right hand has won victory for him,
his holy arm.

R. All the ends of the earth have seen the saving power of God.

The LORD has made his salvation known:
in the sight of the nations he has revealed his justice.
He has remembered his kindness and his faithfulness
toward the house of Israel.

R. All the ends of the earth have seen the saving power of God.

All the ends of the earth have seen
the salvation by our God.
Sing joyfully to the LORD, all you lands;
break into song; sing praise.

R. All the ends of the earth have seen the saving power of God.

ALLELUIA

HEB 1:1-2

R. Alleluia, alleluia.
In times, past, God spoke to our ancestors through the prophets:
in these last days, he has spoken to us through his Son.
R. Alleluia, alleluia.

GOSPEL

Jn 1:19-28

This is the testimony of John.
When the Jews from Jerusalem sent priests and Levites to him
to ask him, "Who are you?"
he admitted and did not deny it, but admitted,
"I am not the Christ."
So they asked him,
"What are you then? Are you Elijah?"
And he said, "I am not."
"Are you the Prophet?"
He answered, "No."
So they said to him,
"Who are you, so we can give an answer to those who sent us?
What do you have to say for yourself?"
He said:
"I am the voice of one crying out in the desert,
'Make straight the way of the Lord,'
as Isaiah the prophet said."
Some Pharisees were also sent.
They asked him,
"Why then do you baptize
if you are not the Christ or Elijah or the Prophet?"
John answered them,
"I baptize with water;
but there is one among you whom you do not recognize,
the one who is coming after me,
whose sandal strap I am not worthy to untie."
This happened in Bethany across the Jordan,
where John was baptizing.

Brothers and sisters, the Gospel of the Lord.

HOMILY:

St. Augustine once wisely said, "In essentials, unity; in non-essentials, liberty; in all things, charity." It might seem like an unrelated statement, but it's profoundly relevant to our understanding of John the Baptist's role. The Jewish leaders were embroiled in debates about titles and positions, but John the Baptist cut through the semantics to reveal the essence of his mission: preparing the way for Christ. He stripped down the non-essentials, focusing solely on charity and love in preparation for the One who would baptize with the Holy Spirit.

Dearly beloved, as we meditate on today's Gospel, let us direct our attention to the humility and clarity of John the Baptist. He was acutely aware of who he was and what his mission entailed. When asked by the Jewish leaders, he did not succumb to pride or indulge in ambiguities. He stated plainly, "I am not the Christ." His self-awareness arose from a deep relationship with God, nourished by solitude and prayer.

In our modern era, it's all too easy to become consumed by titles and social standing. The relentless race for recognition often blinds us to our true calling. Like John the Baptist, we are called to prepare the way for Christ in the lives of those around us. Are we clear about this mission? Do we obscure Christ's light with our pride, or do we, like faithful mirrors, reflect it for all to see?

St. Thomas Aquinas taught that a humble person is more capable of great deeds, not because they underestimate themselves but because they don't underestimate God. Therefore, let us not underestimate the transformative power that humility and self-awareness can have in our lives, especially when rooted in an understanding of God's boundless love and grace.

In these remaining days of the Christmas season, may we seek humility and cultivate self-awareness, not as an end in itself but as a pathway to fulfilling our God-given mission. Amen.

PRAYER:

Gracious and Merciful Father, as we journey through this glorious season of Christmas, we are reminded today through Your servant John the Baptist to be clear in our mission and humble in our hearts. His testimony illuminates the virtue of humility; he understood his role as a voice calling out in the wilderness, paving the way for the coming of Your Son, Jesus Christ, our Savior and Redeemer.

Help us, O Lord, to recognize the areas in our lives where pride may overshadow Your divine work. Fill us with a spirit of humility, much like John the Baptist, so that we may prepare a suitable dwelling place for You within us and among those with whom we interact. Empower us to be clear and honest witnesses of Your truth, and enable us to live out our Christian vocation with deep self-awareness and unconditional love.

In this world where accolades and titles often cloud judgment, enlighten our minds to see the richness of simplicity and the power of self-effacing service. Let us embrace the lesson that it is not our title but our role in Your divine plan that defines us.

As we await the celebration of the Epiphany of our Lord, fill us with the anticipation and joy that marked the journey of the Magi. May we too, like them and like John the Baptist, be led to the Light of the World and respond with awe, reverence, and humble service.

We ask all this in the name of Your Son, our Lord Jesus Christ, who lives and reigns with You and the unity of the Holy Spirit, one God, forever and ever. Amen.

CHRISTMAS WEEKDAY
JANUARY 3

READING 1

1 JN 2:29–3:6

If you consider that God is righteous,
you also know that everyone who acts in righteousness
is begotten by him.
See what love the Father has bestowed on us
that we may be called the children of God.
Yet so we are.
The reason the world does not know us is that it did not know him.
Beloved, we are God's children now;
what we shall be has not yet been revealed.
We do know that when it is revealed we shall be like him,
for we shall see him as he is.
Everyone who has this hope based on him makes himself pure,
as he is pure.
Everyone who commits sin commits lawlessness,
for sin is lawlessness.
You know that he was revealed to take away sins,
and in him there is no sin.
No one who remains in him sins;
no one who sins has seen him or known him.

RESPONSIBLE PSALM

PS 98:1, 3CD-4, 5-6

R. (3cd) All the ends of the earth have seen the saving power of God.
Sing to the LORD a new song,
for he has done wondrous deeds;
His right hand has won victory for him,
his holy arm.

R. All the ends of the earth have seen the saving power of God.

All the ends of the earth have seen
the salvation by our God.
Sing joyfully to the LORD, all you lands;
break into song; sing praise.

R. All the ends of the earth have seen the saving power of God.

Sing praise to the LORD with the harp,
with the harp and melodious song.
With trumpets and the sound of the horn
sing joyfully before the King, the LORD.

R. All the ends of the earth have seen the saving power of God.

ALLELUIA

JN 1:14A, 12A

R. Alleluia, alleluia.
The Word of God became flesh and dwelt among us.
To those who accepted him
he gave power to become the children of God.
R. Alleluia, alleluia.

GOSPEL

Jn 1:29-34

John the Baptist saw Jesus coming toward him and said,
"Behold, the Lamb of God, who takes away the sin of the world.
He is the one of whom I said,
'A man is coming after me who ranks ahead of me
because he existed before me.'
I did not know him,
but the reason why I came baptizing with water
was that he might be made known to Israel."
John testified further, saying,
"I saw the Spirit come down like a dove from the sky
and remain upon him.
I did not know him,
but the one who sent me to baptize with water told me,
'On whomever you see the Spirit come down and remain,
he is the one who will baptize with the Holy Spirit.'
Now I have seen and testified that he is the Son of God."

Brothers and sisters, the Gospel of the Lord.

HOMILY:

St. Augustine once remarked, "Christ is not valued at all unless He is valued above all." This captures the essence of John the Baptist's proclamation: "Behold, the Lamb of God, who takes away the sin of the world!" John the Baptist could have easily clung to his popularity, yet he recognized the unparalleled worth of Christ and steered the attention away from himself and towards Jesus.

My dear brothers and sisters in Christ,

In the Gospel reading of today, we are brought to the banks of the River Jordan where we encounter John the Baptist, a man ablaze with a divine mission. He proclaims, "Behold, the Lamb of God, who takes away the sin of the world!" With these words, he alters the course of human history, offering us the lens through which we are to see and understand Jesus Christ.

What does it mean to call Jesus the "Lamb of God"? In the Old Testament, the lamb was a symbol of sacrifice and deliverance. It harkens back to the Passover, where the blood of the lamb protected the Israelites from the angel of death. Yet, this lamb John points to is unlike any other; it is a lamb that eradicates not just the physical bondage but the spiritual death brought about by sin. In essence, John is introducing the great paradox of the Gospel—the omnipotent God becomes a sacrificial lamb.

In our modern world, consumed by the pursuit of power, status, and material wealth, the image of the "Lamb of God" is counter-intuitive. We often strive to assert ourselves, to dominate and to acquire. Yet, the Gospel calls us to a different kind of assertion—to assert our faith, hope, and love in Jesus, the Lamb who was slain for our redemption. St. Augustine's wisdom, "Christ is not valued at all unless He is valued above all," invites us to prioritize Jesus over our self-interests and worldly pursuits.

As we prepare to celebrate the Epiphany, let us also have our own epiphanies—realizations that turn us towards Christ, the true Light. Let us recalibrate our hearts and minds, ensuring that our lives point, like John the Baptist's did, to Jesus.

May we accept the invitation to witness the Lamb of God in our lives, recognizing that in surrendering to Him, we gain eternal life. It is a call to live not just in adoration of the Lamb, but in emulation of Him—embracing humility, compassion, and sacrifice as we journey through the pathways of our own human wilderness.

Let us be, like John the Baptist, heralds of the Lamb, preparing the way for others to encounter the saving love of Jesus Christ. For in recognizing and proclaiming the Lamb of God, we partake in His divine mission to take away the sins of the world. Amen.

PRAYER:

Heavenly Father, Eternal Light and Source of All Wisdom,

We gather before You today, grateful for the gift of Your Son, Jesus Christ, the Lamb of God who takes away the sin of the world. As we meditate upon the Gospel of John 1:29-34, our hearts are filled with awe and reverence for the mystery You have unfolded for humanity's redemption.

Lord, we recognize the humility and prophetic vision of John the Baptist, who pointed away from himself and towards Jesus, the true Light of the world. Grant us the courage to be heralds like John, illuminating the pathway for others to come to You, as we ourselves strive to follow You more closely each day.

In this Christmas season, prepare our hearts to receive anew the wondrous love You have lavished upon us through Your Son, our Savior. Incline our hearts to realize the value of being both beholden to and a herald of the Lamb of God. As we look forward to celebrating the Epiphany, may our lives be marked by realizations and revelations that draw us closer to You.

Father, we thank You for the grace of encountering You in the liturgy and in our daily lives. We pray for those who have yet to know You, that they may experience the transformative power of Your love.

We offer this prayer in the name of Jesus, the Lamb of God, who, with You and the unity of the Holy Spirit, lives and reigns, one God, forever and ever. Amen.

JANUARY 4

READING 1

1 Jn 3:7-10

Children, let no one deceive you.
The person who acts in righteousness is righteous,
just as he is righteous.
Whoever sins belongs to the Devil,
because the Devil has sinned from the beginning.
Indeed, the Son of God was revealed to destroy the works of the Devil.
No one who is begotten by God commits sin,
because God's seed remains in him;
he cannot sin because he is begotten by God.
In this way,
the children of God and the children of the Devil are made plain;
no one who fails to act in righteousness belongs to God,
nor anyone who does not love his brother.

The word of the Lord.

RESPONSIAL PSALM

Ps 98:1, 7-8, 9

R. (3cd) All the ends of the earth have seen the saving power of God.
Sing to the LORD a new song,
for he has done wondrous deeds;
His right hand has won victory for him,
his holy arm.
R. All the ends of the earth have seen the saving power of God.
Let the sea and what fills it resound,
the world and those who dwell in it;
Let the rivers clap their hands,
the mountains shout with them for joy before the LORD.
R. All the ends of the earth have seen the saving power of God.
The LORD comes;
he comes to rule the earth;
He will rule the world with justice
and the peoples with equity.
R. All the ends of the earth have seen the saving power of God.

ALLELUIA

HEB 1:1-2

R. Alleluia, alleluia.
In the past God spoke to our ancestors through the prophets:
in these last days, he has spoken to us through the Son.
R. Alleluia, alleluia.

GOSPEL

Jn 1:35-42

John was standing with two of his disciples,
and as he watched Jesus walk by, he said,
"Behold, the Lamb of God."
The two disciples heard what he said and followed Jesus.
Jesus turned and saw them following him and said to them,
"What are you looking for?"
They said to him, "Rabbi" (which translated means Teacher),
"where are you staying?"
He said to them, "Come, and you will see."
So they went and saw where he was staying,
and they stayed with him that day.
It was about four in the afternoon.
Andrew, the brother of Simon Peter,
was one of the two who heard John and followed Jesus.
He first found his own brother Simon and told him,
"We have found the Messiah," which is translated Christ.
Then he brought him to Jesus.
Jesus looked at him and said,
"You are Simon the son of John;
you will be called Cephas," which is translated Peter.

Brothers and sisters, the Gospel of the Lord.

HOMILY:

Once, there were two brothers who were struggling artists. One was a sculptor, and the other was a painter. For years they honed their skills without much recognition. One day, a renowned artist came to town and noticed the brothers' extraordinary talents. The acclaimed artist invited them to his studio, offering to teach them and display their works in his gallery. The brothers humbly accepted the invitation, and as they did, their artistry began to flourish in ways they had never before imagined. They went on to impact the world of art profoundly, but they never forgot that it was the invitation and guidance of the one who recognized their talent that made all the difference. Like Andrew and Peter, their lives were changed the day they decided to follow someone who could show them a higher way.

Dear brothers and sisters in Christ,

Today's Gospel from John (1:35-42) speaks of the profound experience of discipleship. Here, we see John the Baptist once again playing the role of one who points the way to Jesus, declaring, "Behold, the Lamb of God!" Andrew and another disciple hear this, and they follow Jesus. Notice that the first words Jesus speaks to them are a question, "What are you looking for?" The disciples answer with another question, "Rabbi, where are you staying?" Jesus simply says, "Come, and you will see."

The beauty of this narrative lies in the simplicity of the invitation and the willingness of the disciples to accept it. Like the brothers in our anecdote, Andrew and Peter's lives were changed when they accepted an invitation from someone who could show them a higher way—the way of love, the way of God. The Gospel today invites us to ask ourselves: Are we willing to follow when Jesus invites us? What are we looking for in our own lives?

In this Christmas season, we are reminded of the greatest invitation ever extended—that of God inviting us into His divine life through the gift of His Son. Just as Andrew and Peter found their purpose and vocation by accepting Jesus' invitation, we too are called to a unique destiny that unfolds when we decide to follow Christ.

As we journey through these last days leading to the celebration of the Epiphany of the Lord, let us prepare our hearts to receive the greatest gift ever given: the gift of God's unconditional love through His Son. May we, like the disciples and like the artist brothers, be willing to drop our nets—the nets of our fears, prejudices, and complacencies—to follow where Jesus leads.

In this spirit, may we find ourselves not merely celebrating the birth of Christ but becoming bearers of Christ, turning our hearts into mangers where the love of God may dwell. Amen.

PRAYER:

Heavenly Father, Creator of heaven and earth,

We come before You in this sacred time of Christmas, filled with awe at the mystery of the Incarnation, the wondrous event where You, our God, have become one of us in Your Son, Jesus Christ.

Today, we reflect upon the Gospel according to John, where Andrew and another disciple heard the calling of John the Baptist to behold the Lamb of God. With hearts open and spirits willing, they followed Jesus, and their lives were transformed forever. We too, Lord, seek to hear Your call in the midst of our everyday lives—calls to love, to serve, to pray, and to sacrifice for the Kingdom of Heaven.

Lord Jesus, just as You asked Andrew and the other disciple, "What are you looking for?" we know that You ask us the same question. Grant us the grace to answer as they did, seeking not just to know about You but to dwell with You. Help us to be ever attentive to Your invitations, however they may come, and give us the courage to respond, "Here I am, Lord; I come to do Your will."

As we anticipate the Feast of the Epiphany, when Your light was shown to all nations, may we too become bearers of that divine light. Let the story of Andrew and Peter inspire us to invite others into Your love, extending the circle of discipleship.

May Your Spirit guide us to live out our baptismal call as true disciples, ever attuned to Your voice, and ever willing to leave behind our worldly concerns to follow You more closely.

In Your most holy name, we pray. Amen.

JANUARY 5

READING 1

1 Jn 3:11-21

Beloved:
This is the message you have heard from the beginning:
we should love one another,
unlike Cain who belonged to the Evil One
and slaughtered his brother.
Why did he slaughter him?
Because his own works were evil,
and those of his brother righteous.
Do not be amazed, then, brothers and sisters, if the world hates you.
We know that we have passed from death to life
because we love our brothers.
Whoever does not love remains in death.
Everyone who hates his brother is a murderer,
and you know that no murderer has eternal life remaining in him.
The way we came to know love
was that he laid down his life for us;
so we ought to lay down our lives for our brothers.
If someone who has worldly means
sees a brother in need and refuses him compassion,
how can the love of God remain in him?
Children, let us love not in word or speech
but in deed and truth.

Now this is how we shall know that we belong to the truth
and reassure our hearts before him
in whatever our hearts condemn,
for God is greater than our hearts and knows everything.
Beloved, if our hearts do not condemn us,
we have confidence in God.

The word of the Lord.

RESPONSORIAL PSALM

PS 100:1b-2, 3, 4, 5

R. (2a) Let all the earth cry out to God with joy.

Sing joyfully to the LORD, all you lands;
serve the LORD with gladness;
come before him with joyful song.

R. Let all the earth cry out to God with joy.

Know that the LORD is God;
he made us, his we are;
his people, the flock he tends.

R. Let all the earth cry out to God with joy.

Enter his gates with thanksgiving,
his courts with praise;
Give thanks to him; bless his name.

R. Let all the earth cry out to God with joy.

The LORD is good:
the LORD, whose kindness endures forever,
and his faithfulness, to all generations.

R. Let all the earth cry out to God with joy.

ALLELUIA

R. Alleluia, alleluia.
A holy day has dawned upon us.
Come, you nations, and adore the Lord.
Today a great light has come upon the earth.
R. Alleluia, alleluia.

GOSPEL

Jn 1:43-51

Jesus decided to go to Galilee, and he found Philip.
And Jesus said to him, "Follow me."
Now Philip was from Bethsaida, the town of Andrew and Peter.
Philip found Nathanael and told him,
"We have found the one about whom Moses wrote in the law,
and also the prophets, Jesus, son of Joseph, from Nazareth."
But Nathanael said to him,
"Can anything good come from Nazareth?"
Philip said to him, "Come and see."
Jesus saw Nathanael coming toward him and said of him,
"Here is a true child of Israel.
There is no duplicity in him."
Nathanael said to him, "How do you know me?"
Jesus answered and said to him,
"Before Philip called you, I saw you under the fig tree."
Nathanael answered him,
"Rabbi, you are the Son of God; you are the King of Israel."
Jesus answered and said to him,
"Do you believe
because I told you that I saw you under the fig tree?
You will see greater things than this."
And he said to him, "Amen, amen, I say to you,
you will see the sky opened and the angels of God
ascending and descending on the Son of Man."

Brothers and sisters, the Gospel of the Lord.

HOMILY:

The story is told of Thomas Merton, the Trappist monk and spiritual writer, who once had a mystical experience at a busy intersection in Louisville, Kentucky. As he stood at the corner of Fourth and Walnut streets, he was suddenly overwhelmed with a profound sense of unity and interconnectedness with all people. "I was suddenly overwhelmed with the realization that I loved all those people, that they were mine and I theirs, that we could not be alien to one another even though we were total strangers." The mystical experience made him realize that we are all connected and united in the gaze of God.

My dear brothers and sisters in Christ,

Today's Gospel reading presents us with the fascinating story of Nathanael and his first encounter with Jesus. It's almost as if Nathanael had a "Fourth and Walnut" experience, as he immediately goes from skepticism to belief. Nathanael starts with a degree of skepticism. "Can anything good come out of Nazareth?" he asks. Yet, within moments of meeting Jesus, he is transformed and declares, "Rabbi, you are the Son of God! You are the King of Israel!"

What changes Nathanael's heart is an authentic encounter with Jesus Christ, an encounter that offers a glimpse of the transcendent reality Merton spoke of. Jesus saw Nathanael under the fig tree even before Philip called him. Jesus sees us in our own 'fig tree moments,' those instances where we think we are alone or hidden from the world. He knows us more deeply than we can comprehend, and he calls us to a relationship with Him.

In a society that often values skepticism and doubt, the conversion of Nathanael is a powerful testament to the impact of an authentic encounter with Jesus. So, as we come closer to the Epiphany of the Lord, let us contemplate how we can experience such authentic encounters and how we can facilitate them for others. Nathanael's story teaches us that a genuine experience with Jesus has the power to transform skepticism into faith, doubt into certainty, and isolation into community.

Therefore, let us be like Philip and extend the invitation, "Come and see." For in extending this invitation, we offer others the greatest gift possible—the opportunity for a transformative encounter with the Son of God, our Savior, Jesus Christ.

May you be blessed in this remaining Christmas season, and may your hearts be prepared to receive the Lord in a new and transformative way as we approach the Feast of the Epiphany. Amen.

PRAYER:

Almighty and Eternal God,

As we continue to celebrate the joyous season of Christmas and prepare our hearts for the radiant feast of the Epiphany, we come before You with hearts full of gratitude and spirits lifted in joyful expectation. Your Word became flesh and dwelt among us, inviting us into an intimate communion with You, just as You invited Nathanael in the Gospel passage we contemplate today.

Lord, we praise You for Your ceaseless gaze upon us, even in our 'fig tree moments' when we feel concealed or isolated. You perceive the depths of our hearts, the authenticity of our faith, and the skepticism that sometimes clouds our vision. May we learn from Nathanael's transformative encounter to always remain open to the mystery of Your divine presence in our lives.

Grant us, O Lord, the courage to extend the invitation to "Come and see" to those around us, especially to those ensnared in doubt or skepticism. May they experience, as Nathanael did, the life-changing power of an authentic encounter with Your Son, Jesus Christ. And may we, like Nathanael, recognize and proclaim Jesus as the Son of God and King of Israel.

In this sacred season, renew in us the gifts of faith, hope, and love, so that we might become worthy witnesses to the Gospel, and like the Wise Men, seek You with undeterred resolve, finding You in the vulnerable and hidden corners of our world.

Through Jesus Christ, our Lord, who lives and reigns with You and the unity of the Holy Spirit, One God, forever and ever.
Amen.

JANUARY 6

READING 1

1 Jn 5:5-13

Beloved:
Who indeed is the victor over the world
but the one who believes that Jesus is the Son of God?

This is the one who came through water and Blood, Jesus Christ,
not by water alone, but by water and Blood.
The Spirit is the one who testifies,
and the Spirit is truth.
So there are three that testify,
the Spirit, the water, and the Blood,
and the three are of one accord.
If we accept human testimony,
the testimony of God is surely greater.
Now the testimony of God is this,
that he has testified on behalf of his Son.
Whoever believes in the Son of God
has this testimony within himself.
Whoever does not believe God has made him a liar
by not believing the testimony God has given about his Son.
And this is the testimony:
God gave us eternal life,
and this life is in his Son.
Whoever possesses the Son has life;
whoever does not possess the Son of God does not have life.

I write these things to you so that you may know
that you have eternal life,
you who believe in the name of the Son of God.
The word of the Lord.

RESPONSORIAL PSALM

PS 147:12-13, 14-15, 19-20

R. (12a) Praise the Lord, Jerusalem.
or:
R. Alleluia.

Glorify the LORD, O Jerusalem;
praise your God, O Zion.
For he has strengthened the bars of your gates;
he has blessed your children within you.

R. Praise the Lord, Jerusalem.
or:
R. Alleluia.

He has granted peace in your borders;
with the best of wheat he fills you.
He sends forth his command to the earth;
swiftly runs his word!

R. Praise the Lord, Jerusalem.
or:
R. Alleluia.

He has proclaimed his word to Jacob,
his statutes and his ordinances to Israel.
He has not done thus for any other nation;
his ordinances he has not made known to them. Alleluia.
R. Praise the Lord, Jerusalem.
or:
R. Alleluia.

ALLELUIA

SEE Mk 9:6

R. Alleluia, alleluia.
The heavens were opened and the voice of the Father thundered:
This is my beloved Son. Listen to him.
R. Alleluia, alleluia.

GOSPEL

Mk 1:7-11

This is what John the Baptist proclaimed:
"One mightier than I is coming after me.
I am not worthy to stoop and loosen the thongs of his sandals.
I have baptized you with water;
he will baptize you with the Holy Spirit."

It happened in those days that Jesus came from Nazareth of Galilee
and was baptized in the Jordan by John.
On coming up out of the water he saw the heavens being torn open
and the Spirit, like a dove, descending upon him.
And a voice came from the heavens,
"You are my beloved Son; with you I am well pleased."

Brothers and sisters, the Gospel of the Lord.

or

Lk 3:23-38

When Jesus began his ministry he was about thirty years of age.
He was the son, as was thought, of Joseph, the son of Heli,
the son of Matthat, the son of Levi, the son of Melchi,
the son of Jannai, the son of Joseph, the son of Mattathias,
the son of Amos, the son of Nahum, the son of Esli,
the son of Naggai, the son of Maath, the son of Mattathias,
the son of Semein, the son of Josech, the son of Joda,
the son of Joanan, the son of Rhesa, the son of Zerubbabel,
the son of Shealtiel, the son of Neri, the son of Melchi,
the son of Addi, the son of Cosam, the son of Elmadam,
the son of Er, the son of Joshua, the son of Eliezer,
the son of Jorim, the son of Matthat, the son of Levi,
the son of Simeon, the son of Judah, the son of Joseph,

the son of Jonam, the son of Eliakim, the son of Melea,
the son of Menna, the son of Mattatha, the son of Nathan,
the son of David, the son of Jesse, the son of Obed,
the son of Boaz, the son of Sala, the son of Nahshon,
the son of Amminadab, the son of Admin, the son of Arni,
the son of Hezron, the son of Perez, the son of Judah,
the son of Jacob, the son of Isaac, the son of Abraham,
the son of Terah, the son of Nahor, the son of Serug,
the son of Reu, the son of Peleg, the son of Eber,
the son of Shelah, the son of Cainan, the son of Arphaxad,
the son of Shem, the son of Noah, the son of Lamech,
the son of Methuselah, the son of Enoch, the son of Jared,
the son of Mahalaleel, the son of Cainan, the son of Enos,
the son of Seth, the son of Adam, the son of God.

or

Lk 3:23, 31-34, 36, 38

When Jesus began his ministry he was about thirty years of age.
He was the son, as was thought, of Joseph, the son of Heli,
the son of Melea, the son of Menna, the son of Mattatha,
the son of Nathan, the son of David, the son of Jesse,
the son of Obed, the son of Boaz, the son of Sala,
the son of Nahshon, the son of Amminadab, the son of Admin,
the son of Arni, the son of Hezron, the son of Perez,
the son of Judah, the son of Jacob, the son of Isaac,
the son of Abraham, the son of Terah, the son of Nahor,
the son of Cainan, the son of Arphaxad, the son of Shem,
the son of Noah, the son of Lamech, the son of Enos,
the son of Seth, the son of Adam, the son of God.

HOMILY:

The ancient ritual of Baptism in the Christian tradition is more than a mere formality; it is a profound moment that signifies a radical transformation. An apt metaphor might be that of the chrysalis transforming into a butterfly. For the butterfly, the old life is gone, and a new, gloriously transformed existence begins. Like the butterfly, those who are baptized emerge from the waters not merely cleaned but profoundly changed. This transformative power of baptism can be seen in the lives of countless saints and holy men and women throughout history.

Dear brothers and sisters in Christ,

Today's Gospel from Mark (1:7-11) recounts the baptism of Jesus—a pivotal moment that marks the beginning of His public ministry. John the Baptist, the forerunner, proclaims the arrival of One greater than himself, so great that John feels unworthy even to stoop down and untie His sandals. Yet, it is Jesus who humbles Himself to be baptized by John.

Let us ponder the significance of this paradox: the eternal Son of God, free from sin, submits to the baptism of repentance. What does this tell us? It reminds us that humility and obedience are at the core of divine love. St. Augustine of Hippo once observed, "Christ is baptized, not to be made holy by the water, but to make the water holy." Through His baptism, Christ sanctifies the waters, making it an instrument of divine grace for us all.

The heavens themselves part at the baptism of Jesus, and the voice of the Father declares, "You are my beloved Son; with you I am well pleased." Here we find a Trinitarian revelation: The Father's voice from heaven, the Son's submission in the Jordan, and the Holy Spirit descending like a dove. In this divine exchange, we glimpse the ineffable unity and diversity in the Godhead—a mystery to which our own sacrament of baptism baptism of Jesus is not just a historical event but a living lesson for our spiritual journey. Just as the Spirit descended upon Jesus, so too does the Spirit descend upon us in our own baptism, confirming us as children of God and equipping us for the mission of Christian life. It is essential, especially in these conforms us.

The modern times fraught with secularism and spiritual apathy, to remember and renew the vows of our baptism regularly.

In the words of St. Thomas Aquinas, "Through Baptism we are made flesh of the Crucified." We are called not just to admire Jesus but to follow Him, to carry our crosses, to live with integrity, and to act justly.

Let us strive to be worthy of our calling, recognizing that we, too, are God's beloved children, and He is well pleased when we live in a manner that reflects His love and wisdom. Amen.

PRAYER:

Heavenly Father,

We gather before You in humble adoration and gratitude, mindful of Your abundant blessings and unconditional love. As we contemplate the Gospel of Mark 1:7-11, we are profoundly moved by the baptism of Your beloved Son, Jesus Christ, in the River Jordan. This sacramental moment of divine revelation illuminates the extraordinary beauty of Your Trinitarian presence: the Father speaking from heaven, the Son submitting in humility, and the Holy Spirit descending like a dove.

Oh God, who sanctified the waters of the Jordan through the baptism of Your Son, we beseech You to sanctify us. Renew in us the graces of our own baptism, the pledge of faith that we may have received as infants or at a mature age, but which needs constant nurturing. Let Your Holy Spirit, who descended upon Your Son, continue to guide us in discerning Your will in our lives.

Lord, as St. Augustine of Hippo marvelously proclaimed, Christ was not baptized to be sanctified by water, but to sanctify the water itself. May we, too, become instruments of sanctification in this world, sanctifying our own environments through acts of love, mercy, and justice. And just as Your voice rang out, declaring Your pleasure in Your Son, may our lives be a pleasing offering to You.

In this modern world, replete with distractions and complexities, grant us the spiritual fortitude to live out our baptismal promises courageously. Let us never forget that we are Your children, chosen and cherished, destined not for the fleeting pleasures of this world, but for eternal union with You.

Through the intercession of all the saints, who have lived out their baptismal vows to the full, especially the likes of St. Thomas Aquinas, who beautifully expounded on the sacraments, we pray that we may live as worthy disciples of Christ.

We ask this through Christ, our Lord. Amen.

JANUARY 7

READING 1

1 Jn 5:14-21

Beloved:
We have this confidence in God,
that if we ask anything according to his will, he hears us.
And if we know that he hears us in regard to whatever we ask,
we know that what we have asked him for is ours.
If anyone sees his brother sinning, if the sin is not deadly,
he should pray to God and he will give him life.
This is only for those whose sin is not deadly.
There is such a thing as deadly sin,
about which I do not say that you should pray.
All wrongdoing is sin, but there is sin that is not deadly.

We know that no one begotten by God sins;
but the one begotten by God he protects,
and the Evil One cannot touch him.
We know that we belong to God,
and the whole world is under the power of the Evil One.
We also know that the Son of God has come
and has given us discernment to know the one who is true.
And we are in the one who is true, in his Son Jesus Christ.
He is the true God and eternal life.
Children, be on your guard against idols.

The word of the Lord.

RESPONSORIAL PSALM

Ps 149:1-2, 3-4, 5 and 6a and 9b

R. (see 4a) The Lord takes delight in his people.
or:
R. Alleluia.

Sing to the LORD a new song
of praise in the assembly of the faithful.
Let Israel be glad in their maker,
let the children of Zion rejoice in their king.

R. The Lord takes delight in his people.
or:
R. Alleluia.

Let them praise his name in the festive dance,
let them sing praise to him with timbrel and harp.
For the LORD loves his people,
and he adorns the lowly with victory.

R. The Lord takes delight in his people.
or:
R. Alleluia.

Let the faithful exult in glory;
let them sing for joy upon their couches;
Let the high praises of God be in their throats.
This is the glory of all his faithful. Alleluia.

R. The Lord takes delight in his people.
or:
R. Alleluia.

ALLELUIA

Lk 7:16

R. Alleluia, alleluia.
A great prophet has arisen in our midst
and God has visited his people.
R. Alleluia, alleluia.

GOSPEL

Jn 2:1-11

There was a wedding at Cana in Galilee,
and the mother of Jesus was there.
Jesus and his disciples were also invited to the wedding.
When the wine ran short,
the mother of Jesus said to him,
"They have no wine."
And Jesus said to her,
"Woman, how does your concern affect me?
My hour has not yet come."
His mother said to the servers,
"Do whatever he tells you."
Now there were six stone water jars there for Jewish ceremonial washings,
each holding twenty to thirty gallons.
Jesus told them,
"Fill the jars with water."
So they filled them to the brim.
Then he told them,
"Draw some out now and take it to the headwaiter."
So they took it.
And when the headwaiter tasted the water that had become wine,
without knowing where it came from
(although the servers who had drawn the water knew),
the headwaiter called the bridegroom and said to him,
"Everyone serves good wine first,
and then when people have drunk freely, an inferior one;
but you have kept the good wine until now."
Jesus did this as the beginning of his signs at Cana in Galilee
and so revealed his glory,
and his disciples began to believe in him.

Brothers and sisters, the Gospel of the Lord.

HOMILY:

In the 13th century, St. Thomas Aquinas was once invited by Pope Urban IV to a feast. The holy theologian was deep in thought about the mysteries of the Eucharist, seemingly absent from the worldly celebrations around him. Suddenly, he came to some profound theological realization and muttered some notes on the parchment beside him. Sensing something extraordinary, the Pope asked Thomas what it was. St. Thomas told the Pope about his new understanding of the Eucharistic mystery. Pope Urban IV was so moved that he reportedly said, "Thomas, you have written well of the sacrament of My Body," invoking the words Christ might have said.

This brings us to the Gospel of John (2:1-11) the Wedding Feast at Cana. Like the Pope's feast, it was a setting of joy and celebration. However, amid the festivities, something extraordinary happened: water was turned into wine. The transformation that occurred at Cana offers an avenue for theological and practical contemplation, much like St. Thomas Aquinas' Eucharistic contemplations.

Dear brothers and sisters in Christ,

As we navigate the season of Christmas towards the Epiphany of the Lord, the Gospel presents us with a remarkable event—the first of Jesus' signs, the transformation of water into wine at a wedding feast in Cana.

Here we are given a rich tapestry of symbolism and meaning that far exceeds the simple narrative. Just as St. Thomas Aquinas delved into the profound mysteries of the sacraments during a feast, we too are invited to delve deeply into this Gospel, which speaks volumes about the nature of God's intervention in our lives.

Firstly, consider the setting: a wedding, a union, an earthly representation of the heavenly banquet we all aspire to attend. Jesus, Mary, and the disciples are all present, underscoring the significance of human relationships blessed by divine presence.

Secondly, ponder the problem: the wine has run out. It is not a life-threatening crisis, but it is a social embarrassment, a diminishment of joy. Mary, ever attentive, brings this to Jesus. Her concern is our concern—those daily needs, small yet significant, that disrupt our peace and happiness. And what is Jesus' response? He transforms ordinary water into extraordinary wine.

In this miraculous transformation, we witness a foreshadowing of the ultimate transformation—the Eucharist. The ordinary elements of bread and wine are turned into the Body and Blood of Christ, much like St. Thomas Aquinas pondered upon. It's a transformation that not only honors God but elevates humanity, pulling us into the divine life.

Lastly, notice the quality of the wine. It is not just any wine but choice wine. God's grace is not mediocre; it's extraordinary. When God acts, He surpasses all expectations. In our modern world, filled with both marvels and disappointments, this Gospel narrative reminds us that God's grace is continually poured into our lives, transforming our 'water' into 'wine'—our ordinary into extraordinary, our humanity into divinity.

May we, like Mary, be attentive to those in need. May we, like the servants at Cana, obey the Lord's commands. And may we, like St. Thomas Aquinas, be ever attentive to the deeper mysteries that everyday events can reveal, for in them lies the extraordinary grace of God.

In Christ's love and peace, Amen.

PRAYER:

Heavenly Father, Author of all good things, as we continue in this season of Christmas towards the majestic feast of the Epiphany, we come before You with hearts filled with gratitude and awe. We are moved by the Gospel narrative of the Wedding Feast at Cana, where Your Son, our Lord Jesus Christ, performed His first public miracle—transforming simple water into choice wine.

Lord, in this act, we see a glimmer of Your endless love and extraordinary grace. We recognize the profundity of small acts performed with great love, and how Your presence elevates them. As St. Thomas Aquinas explored the extraordinary within the ordinary through his ponderings on the Eucharist, may we too perceive Your miracles in our daily lives, both big and small.

Incline our hearts to be like Mary, observant and attentive to the needs around us. Empower us to be like the servants, obedient and trusting in Your word. Above all, grant us the wisdom to see that even in the most mundane aspects of our lives, You are working to transform our 'water' into 'wine'—our ordinary into extraordinary, our struggles into triumphs.

May this miracle at Cana remind us that You are not a God of scarcity but of abundance, not of mere adequacy but of excellence. You do not just fill our cups, Lord; You make them overflow.

As we await the Epiphany of the Lord, brighten the eyes of our hearts so that we may see Your glory manifest in our lives. Let the miracle at Cana fortify our faith, making us ever mindful of Your constant work of transformation within us and the world.

Through Christ, our Lord, Amen.

OR JANUARY 7
MONDAY AFTER EPIPHANY

READING 1

1 Jn 3:22–4:6

Beloved:
We receive from him whatever we ask,
because we keep his commandments and do what pleases him.
And his commandment is this:
we should believe in the name of his Son, Jesus Christ,
and love one another just as he commanded us.
Those who keep his commandments remain in him, and he in them,
and the way we know that he remains in us
is from the Spirit whom he gave us.

Beloved, do not trust every spirit
but test the spirits to see whether they belong to God,
because many false prophets have gone out into the world.
This is how you can know the Spirit of God:
every spirit that acknowledges Jesus Christ come in the flesh
belongs to God,
and every spirit that does not acknowledge Jesus
does not belong to God.
This is the spirit of the antichrist
who, as you heard, is to come,
but in fact is already in the world.
You belong to God, children, and you have conquered them,
for the one who is in you
is greater than the one who is in the world.
They belong to the world;
accordingly, their teaching belongs to the world,
and the world listens to them.
We belong to God, and anyone who knows God listens to us,
while anyone who does not belong to God refuses to hear us.

This is how we know the spirit of truth and the spirit of deceit.

The word of the Lord.

RESPONSORIAL PSALM

Ps 2:7bc-8, 10-12a

R. (8ab) I will give you all the nations for an inheritance.

The LORD said to me, "You are my Son;
this day I have begotten you.
Ask of me and I will give you
the nations for an inheritance
and the ends of the earth for your possession."

R. I will give you all the nations for an inheritance.

And now, O kings, give heed;
take warning, you rulers of the earth.
Serve the LORD with fear, and rejoice before him;
with trembling rejoice.

R. I will give you all the nations for an inheritance.

GOSPEL

Mt 4:12-17, 23-25

When Jesus heard that John had been arrested,
he withdrew to Galilee.
He left Nazareth and went to live in Capernaum by the sea,
in the region of Zebulun and Naphtali,
that what had been said through Isaiah the prophet
might be fulfilled:

Land of Zebulun and land of Naphtali,
the way to the sea, beyond the Jordan,
Galilee of the Gentiles,
the people who sit in darkness
have seen a great light,
on those dwelling in a land overshadowed by death
light has arisen.

From that time on, Jesus began to preach and say,
"Repent, for the Kingdom of heaven is at hand."

He went around all of Galilee,
teaching in their synagogues, proclaiming the Gospel of the Kingdom,
and curing every disease and illness among the people.
His fame spread to all of Syria,
and they brought to him all who were sick with various diseases
and racked with pain,
those who were possessed, lunatics, and paralytics,
and he cured them.
And great crowds from Galilee, the Decapolis, Jerusalem, and Judea,
and from beyond the Jordan followed him.

Brothers and sisters, the Gospel of the Lord.

HOMILY:

In the early days of Christianity, St. Augustine, one of the greatest theologians and philosophers, was once accosted by a pagan who showed him his idol and said, "Here is my god; where is yours?" Augustine replied, "I cannot show you my God; not because there is no God to show but because you have no eyes to see Him."

Dear brothers and sisters in Christ,

As we transition from the splendor of the Epiphany, we are presented today with the Gospel of Matthew, chapter 4, verses 12 to 17, and 23 to 25. In these passages, we see Jesus emerging from the shadow cast by the imprisonment of John the Baptist. The light of Christ begins to shine brightly, penetrating the lives of those in Galilee, fulfilling the prophecy of Isaiah: "the people who sat in darkness have seen a great light."

Today, we find ourselves in similar situations where darkness prevails. This darkness isn't merely physical; it's a spiritual, moral, and emotional darkness that often overshadows our lives—whether it's the weight of sin, the disillusionment of societal woes, or the private struggles that burden our hearts. But take courage, for the Gospel assures us that the same Light that shone in Galilee is here, now, ready to illuminate our lives.

St. Augustine's exchange with the pagan is emblematic of our own spiritual myopia. Often, we are blind to the Divine Light that seeks to penetrate our lives. We are caught in the trivialities and immediate urgencies that we forget to look for the Light. But remember, Christ did not only come to shine His Light in our lives; He came to give us eyes that we might see. As St. Augustine profoundly expressed, it's not the absence of God that's the issue; it's our inability to recognize Him.

Christ's ministry was not limited to sermons; it was holistic—preaching, teaching, and healing. The Light of Christ aims to touch every facet of our being. Let us, therefore, open our hearts, lift our moral gaze, and refocus our spiritual vision to perceive the Light that Christ offers. As disciples, our mission doesn't end in seeing the Light; we are called to become beacons of this Divine Light.

May the words of Christ in today's Gospel, "Repent, for the kingdom of heaven has come near," serve as a constant reminder for us to turn away from our old ways, making room for the Light that transforms. Let us be like St. Augustine, not just seekers of the Divine but witnesses to it, aiding others in removing the scales from their eyes to behold the great Light that has dawned upon us. Amen.

PRAYER:

Almighty and Everlasting God, who hast revealed Thyself in the radiant Light of the Incarnation, we gather in humility and gratitude as we continue to contemplate the profound mystery of the Epiphany.

In the Gospel of Matthew, we have heard today how Your Son, our Lord Jesus Christ, commenced His earthly ministry in the wake of John the Baptist's imprisonment. With great compassion and fervor, He shined His Light into the lives of those dwelling in the darkness of Galilee. Today, we beseech You to shine that same Light into our lives and into the darkness of our modern world.

Grant us, we pray, the spiritual eyesight to recognize Your active presence in our lives. May we repent for our transgressions, our lapses in judgment, and our moral failures, and so prepare the way for Your Kingdom to be established in our hearts. As Your Son healed all manner of infirmities among the people, may He heal us too—spiritually, emotionally, and physically.

O Lord, empower us to be not only recipients of Your illuminating grace but also its conduits. Let our lives be so transformed by Your Light that we may become beacons of hope, justice, and love to those around us, just as St. Augustine was in his time.

In the name of Your Son, Jesus Christ, who lives and reigns with You and the unity of the Holy Spirit, one God, forever and ever. Amen.

JANUARY 8
TUESDAY AFTER EPIPHANY

Reading 1 1 Jn 4:7-10

Beloved, let us love one another,
because love is of God;
everyone who loves is begotten by God and knows God.
Whoever is without love does not know God, for God is love.
In this way the love of God was revealed to us:
God sent his only-begotten Son into the world
so that we might have life through him.
In this is love:
not that we have loved God, but that he loved us
and sent his Son as expiation for our sins.

The word of the Lord.

RESPONSORIAL PSALM

Ps 72:1-2, 3-4, 7-8

R. (see 11) Lord, every nation on earth will adore you.

O God, with your judgment endow the king,
and with your justice, the king's son;
He shall govern your people with justice
and your afflicted ones with judgment.

R. Lord, every nation on earth will adore you.

The mountains shall yield peace for the people,
and the hills justice.
He shall defend the afflicted among the people,
save the children of the poor.

R. Lord, every nation on earth will adore you.

Justice shall flower in his days,
and profound peace, till the moon be no more.
May he rule from sea to sea,
and from the River to the ends of the earth.

R. Lord, every nation on earth will adore you.

GOSPEL

Mk 6:34-44

When Jesus saw the vast crowd, his heart was moved with pity for them,
for they were like sheep without a shepherd;
and he began to teach them many things.
By now it was already late and his disciples approached him and said,
"This is a deserted place and it is already very late.
Dismiss them so that they can go
to the surrounding farms and villages
and buy themselves something to eat."
He said to them in reply,
"Give them some food yourselves."
But they said to him,
"Are we to buy two hundred days' wages worth of food
and give it to them to eat?"
He asked them, "How many loaves do you have? Go and see."
And when they had found out they said,
"Five loaves and two fish."
So he gave orders to have them sit down in groups on the green grass.
The people took their places in rows by hundreds and by fifties.
Then, taking the five loaves and the two fish and looking up to heaven,
he said the blessing, broke the loaves, and gave them to his disciples
to set before the people;
he also divided the two fish among them all.
They all ate and were satisfied.
And they picked up twelve wicker baskets full of fragments
and what was left of the fish.
Those who ate of the loaves were five thousand men.

Brothers and sisters, the Gospel of the Lord.

HOMILY:

St. John Chrysostom, the Early Church Father and Archbishop of Constantinople, once spoke profoundly on the significance of the feeding of the multitudes. He emphasized not just the miracle of multiplication but also the discipline and faith required of the apostles to distribute what seemed insufficient. "See how the miracle is interwoven with human effort," he said, reminding us that even divine action involves human participation.

My dear brothers and sisters in Christ,

Today's Gospel narrative is among the most vivid and inspiring in all of Sacred Scripture: The feeding of the five thousand in Mark (6:34-44.) In a barren place, faced with a multitude of hungry souls, Jesus performed a miracle that transcended mere nourishment of the body; it was a feast for the soul, an Epiphany of divine providence and compassion.

The story begins with Jesus moved by the sight of a "large crowd, like sheep without a shepherd." This image alone carries immense weight, for we live in an era that mirrors this biblical description—a world where many are lost, confused, and spiritually hungry, yearning for guidance, moral clarity, and, above all, love.

What does Jesus do? He "began to teach them many things," thereby tending first to their spiritual hunger. Isn't it a reminder for us that, even in our most dire needs, spiritual nourishment comes before the material? As Jesus later taught, "Man shall not live by bread alone."

The miracle that follows is rich with symbolism and theological depth. Jesus takes the five loaves and two fish—utterly insufficient to human eyes—and multiplies them to feed thousands. Just as St. John Chrysostom observed, this divine action also involved human cooperation. The disciples had to trust Jesus enough to start distributing the scant food they had. It's a lesson for us, too, in the Christian life. Faith is not a passive receiving but an active collaboration with God's grace.

And so, we are all called to be both recipients and distributors of this miraculous love, this extraordinary grace, that turns scarcity into abundance. We are to be co-workers with Christ, aware that even our most modest offerings can become monumental when touched by the divine.

In this modern age, with its unique challenges and complexities, let us remember the power of Christ to multiply not just bread and fish but hope, love, and grace. May our own lives, in concert with divine grace, become a feast that feeds both body and spirit, quenching the deepest hungers of our brothers and sisters.

May God's peace and blessings be upon you all. Amen.

PRAYER:

Almighty and Everlasting Father,

As we gather here today, our hearts reflect upon the miraculous feeding of the five thousand as recounted in the Gospel of Mark. We are moved by Your divine compassion for the hungry multitude, a compassion that extends beyond the needs of the body to the longings of the soul.

Gracious God, just as You multiplied the five loaves and two fish, we humbly ask that You multiply the good works and intentions of our own hands. Teach us to trust in Your limitless providence, especially when faced with seemingly insurmountable odds. May we ever remember that, when united with Your grace, even our modest offerings can effect profound transformations.

Inspire in us, O Lord, a spirit of service and stewardship, so that we might become active collaborators in Your eternal plan. May we, like Your disciples of old, distribute Your boundless love and mercy to all we encounter—feeding the hungry, comforting the distressed, and providing spiritual nourishment to those who thirst for truth and righteousness.

We also pray for those among us who are suffering, whether from physical need, emotional pain, or spiritual emptiness. Grant them the fullness of Your peace and meet them in their need, just as You met the needs of the crowd on that day in Galilee.

Through the intercession of all the saints and guided by the Holy Spirit, we offer this prayer in the name of Your Son, our Lord Jesus Christ, who lives and reigns with You forever and ever. Amen.

JANUARY 9
WEDNESDAY AFTER EPIPHANY

READING 1

1 Jn 4:11-18

Beloved, if God so loved us,
we also must love one another.
No one has ever seen God.
Yet, if we love one another, God remains in us,
and his love is brought to perfection in us.

This is how we know that we remain in him and he in us,
that he has given us of his Spirit.
Moreover, we have seen and testify
that the Father sent his Son as savior of the world.
Whoever acknowledges that Jesus is the Son of God,
God remains in him and he in God.
We have come to know and to believe in the love God has for us.

God is love, and whoever remains in love remains in God and God in him.
In this is love brought to perfection among us,
that we have confidence on the day of judgment
because as he is, so are we in this world.
There is no fear in love,
but perfect love drives out fear
because fear has to do with punishment,
and so one who fears is not yet perfect in love.

The word of the Lord

RESPONSORIAL PSALM

Ps 72:1-2, 10, 12-13

R. (see 11) Lord, every nation on earth will adore you.

O God, with your judgment endow the king,
and with your justice, the king's son;
He shall govern your people with justice
and your afflicted ones with judgment.

R. Lord, every nation on earth will adore you.

The kings of Tarshish and the Isles shall offer gifts;
the kings of Arabia and Seba shall bring tribute.

R. Lord, every nation on earth will adore you.

For he shall rescue the poor when he cries out,
and the afflicted when he has no one to help him.
He shall have pity for the lowly and the poor;
the lives of the poor he shall save.

R. Lord, every nation on earth will adore you.

GOSPEL

Mk 6:45-52

After the five thousand had eaten and were satisfied,
Jesus made his disciples get into the boat
and precede him to the other side toward Bethsaida,
while he dismissed the crowd.
And when he had taken leave of them,
he went off to the mountain to pray.
When it was evening,
the boat was far out on the sea and he was alone on shore.
Then he saw that they were tossed about while rowing,
for the wind was against them.
About the fourth watch of the night,
he came toward them walking on the sea.
He meant to pass by them.
But when they saw him walking on the sea,
they thought it was a ghost and cried out.
They had all seen him and were terrified.
But at once he spoke with them,
"Take courage, it is I, do not be afraid!"
He got into the boat with them and the wind died down.
They were completely astounded.
They had not understood the incident of the loaves.
On the contrary, their hearts were hardened.

Brothers and sister, the Gospel of the Lord.

HOMILY:

Many years ago, there was a man named Paul who was an expert sailor. He had a younger brother, Mark, who had never been out on the water. Wanting to share his love for sailing, Paul invited Mark to join him on a boat trip across a large lake. As they set sail, the skies were clear, and the waters were calm. Yet, halfway through the journey, they were caught in an unexpected storm. Mark was terrified, but Paul, understanding the intricacies of sailing, remained calm and navigated them safely to shore. Mark, reflecting on the experience, later realized that it was not just the boat that kept them afloat, but the expertise and calm of his older brother.

Dear brothers and sisters in Christ,

Today's Gospel according to Mark speaks of another storm—a storm on the Sea of Galilee where the disciples find themselves battling winds and waves in the middle of the night. Christ walks toward them on water, uttering the timeless assurance: "Take courage, it is I, do not be afraid."

Firstly, let us contemplate the significance of Jesus walking on water. This is more than a spectacle; it's a revelation of His divine nature. Jesus' action shows His mastery over the natural elements, symbolizing His dominion over all earthly troubles and spiritual forces that would seek to subvert our faith.

We can draw an analogy between this Gospel story and the story of Paul and Mark. The disciples are like Mark, fearful and inexperienced in navigating the challenges that life's storms throw at them. Jesus, much like Paul, approaches them in their hour of need to guide and reassure.

How often do we find ourselves in a tempest of confusion, doubt, or despair? Like the disciples and Mark, our immediate reaction might be fear. But let us remember, Christ walks into our lives at these moments, telling us, "It is I, do not be afraid." Our faith, fortified by the understanding that Christ is the Master of our destinies, becomes the vessel that allows us to weather the storm.

So, let us pray for the courage to trust Him, particularly when the winds are contrary and the waves are high. Christ, our eternal lighthouse, navigates us safely through every storm, leading us to the calm shores of faith and the eternal embrace of His love.

Saint Augustine once said, "Faith is to believe what you do not see; the reward of this faith is to see what you believe." May we have the faith to believe in Christ's presence in our lives, so that, guided by this faith, we may see His loving providence in all things. Amen.

PRAYER:

Heavenly Father, Creator of Heaven and Earth, and the God of calm amid storms,

Today we have gathered to reflect on Your holy Gospel according to Mark, wherein Jesus walks on water and calms the fears of His disciples. We thank You for this timeless lesson, a testament to Your unbounded power and unwavering love for each of us.

Lord, we ask for the grace to always recognize Your divine presence, especially in the storms of our lives, whether they be physical, emotional, or spiritual. Just as the disciples were filled with awe when they witnessed Your power, fill our hearts with awe and faith to trust in Your divine providence in all circumstances.

Father, grant us the courage to step out in faith, even when the winds are contrary and the waves are high. May we remember that You are ever near, whispering, "Take courage, it is I, do not be afraid." Help us to internalize this eternal promise, so that fear may have no dominion over us.

We lift up all those facing storms in their lives right now—those struggling with illness, despair, loss, or doubt. May they feel Your comforting presence and come to a deeper understanding of Your infinite love and power.

Saint Augustine told us that faith is the act of believing in what we cannot see, and the reward of this faith is to see what we have believed in. May our faith guide us to the serene and safe harbors of Your love, through the merits of Jesus Christ, our Lord and Savior.

In Your holy and blessed name, we pray. Amen.

JANUARY 10
THURSDAY AFTER EPIPHANY

READING 1

1 Jn 4:19–5:4

Beloved, we love God because
he first loved us.
If anyone says, "I love God,"
but hates his brother, he is a liar;
for whoever does not love a brother whom he has seen
cannot love God whom he has not seen.
This is the commandment we have from him:
Whoever loves God must also love his brother.

Everyone who believes that Jesus is the Christ is begotten by God,
and everyone who loves the Father
loves also the one begotten by him.
In this way we know that we love the children of God
when we love God and obey his commandments.
For the love of God is this,
that we keep his commandments.
And his commandments are not burdensome,
for whoever is begotten by God conquers the world.
And the victory that conquers the world is our faith.

The word of the Lord.

JANUARY 10 THURSDAY AFTER EPIPHANY

RESPONSORIAL PSALM

Ps 72:1-2, 14 and 15bc, 17

R. (see 11) Lord, every nation on earth will adore you.

O God, with your judgment endow the king,
and with your justice, the king's son;
He shall govern your people with justice
and your afflicted ones with judgment.

R. Lord, every nation on earth will adore you.

From fraud and violence he shall redeem them,
and precious shall their blood be in his sight.
May they be prayed for continually;
day by day shall they bless him.

R. Lord, every nation on earth will adore you.

May his name be blessed forever;
as long as the sun his name shall remain.
In him shall all the tribes of the earth be blessed;
all the nations shall proclaim his happiness.

R. Lord, every nation on earth will adore you.

GOSPEL

Lk 4:14-22

Jesus returned to Galilee in the power of the Spirit,
and news of him spread throughout the whole region.
He taught in their synagogues and was praised by all.

He came to Nazareth, where he had grown up,
and went according to his custom
into the synagogue on the sabbath day.
He stood up to read and was handed a scroll of the prophet Isaiah.
He unrolled the scroll and found the passage where it was written:
The Spirit of the Lord is upon me,
because he has anointed me
to bring glad tidings to the poor.

He has sent me to proclaim liberty to captives
and recovery of sight to the blind,
to let the oppressed go free,
and to proclaim a year acceptable to the Lord.

Rolling up the scroll, he handed it back to the attendant and sat down,
and the eyes of all in the synagogue looked intently at him.
He said to them,
"Today this Scripture passage is fulfilled in your hearing."
And all spoke highly of him
and were amazed at the gracious words that came from his mouth.

Brothers and sisters, the Gospel of the Lord.

HOMILY:

In the medieval period, Saint Thomas Aquinas was invited to dine with King Louis IX of France, who held the learned saint in high regard. During the meal, the conversation turned to the profundities of theology and scripture. Completely absorbed, St. Thomas suddenly slammed his fist onto the table, as if struck by an epiphany, exclaiming, "That will settle the Manichees!" The king, so inspired by Thomas's genuine enthusiasm for truth, immediately ordered a scribe to document Thomas's insight, which had the potential to refute a prevalent heresy of his time.

Beloved in Christ,

In today's Gospel according to Luke, we read of Jesus returning to Galilee, "in the power of the Spirit." He goes into the synagogue, as was His custom, and reads from the scroll of the prophet Isaiah: "The Spirit of the Lord is upon me, because he has anointed me to bring glad tidings to the poor."

This moment is a profound epiphany of its own, signifying Jesus's public declaration of His mission. It encapsulates His role as prophet, priest, and king, and encompasses a mission of liberation, healing, and proclamation of the year of the Lord's favor. Then, with everyone's eyes fixed on Him, He declares, "Today this Scripture passage is fulfilled in your hearing."

In the same way that Saint Thomas Aquinas was consumed with a zeal for God's truth, we too are called to be impassioned disciples of the Gospel. The call to spread the Good News is not limited to prophets, apostles, or saints but is a mandate for every baptized Christian.

However, let us not overlook the reality that Jesus's proclamation was met with wonder, but also led to skepticism among those who had seen Him grow up. They questioned, "Is this not Joseph's son?" We, too, may face skepticism or rejection when we choose to speak and live out the Gospel. Yet, Jesus did not waver in His mission, and neither should we. The power of the Spirit that Jesus felt is the same Spirit given to us in our Baptism and Confirmation.

The life of Saint Thomas Aquinas teaches us that insights and revelations should be used for the service of the Church and for the glory of God. Like him, we must use our talents and understanding in the propagation of faith and for the welfare of the community.

Let us remember that Jesus's mission is now our mission. In the words of the philosopher Søren Kierkegaard, "Christ turned water into wine, but the church has succeeded in doing something even more difficult: it has turned wine into water." May we turn the 'water' back into 'wine' by living a life in accordance with the Gospel, filled with the exuberance of faith and the richness of God's love. Thus, may we truly proclaim the year of the Lord's favor, today and every day. Amen.

PRAYER:

Heavenly Father, we come before You today, rejoicing in the luminous feast of the Epiphany that still bathes us in its light. We stand in awe of the Word made flesh, Your Son, our Lord Jesus Christ, who has come to bring glad tidings to the poor, to proclaim liberty to captives, and give sight to the blind.

As we meditate on today's Gospel, where Jesus unfurls the scroll to announce His God-given mission, may we too be inspired to discern and declare our own missions as Your disciples. Fill us, we pray, with the Holy Spirit that filled Christ, so that we may recognize our anointing not as a privilege but as a responsibility— to bring justice to the oppressed, offer love to the marginalized, and hope to those entrenched in despair.

Father, we are often like those in the synagogue, amazed but skeptical, trapped in our limited perceptions and worldly judgments. Shake us from our doubts, embolden us in our faith, and guide us in our actions, so that the words of Isaiah may be fulfilled not just in the hearing but in the doing, transforming the 'today' of this moment into an eternal now of Divine Love and Mercy.

May we draw inspiration from the dedication of Saint Thomas Aquinas and other luminous figures in Your Church, who used their gifts and epiphanies to serve Your kingdom. In this, may we, like them, turn our moments of profound understanding into a lifetime of service.

Through Jesus Christ, our Savior and Redeemer, who lives and reigns with You and the unity of the Holy Spirit, one God, forever and ever. Amen.

JANUARY 11
FRIDAY AFTER EPIPHANY

READING 1
1 Jn 5:5-13

Beloved:
Who indeed is the victor over the world
but the one who believes that Jesus is the Son of God?

This is the one who came through water and Blood, Jesus Christ,
not by water alone, but by water and Blood.
The Spirit is the one who testifies,
and the Spirit is truth.
So there are three who testify,
the Spirit, the water, and the Blood,
and the three are of one accord.
If we accept human testimony,
the testimony of God is surely greater.
Now the testimony of God is this,
that he has testified on behalf of his Son.
Whoever believes in the Son of God
has this testimony within himself.
Whoever does not believe God has made him a liar
by not believing the testimony God has given about his Son.
And this is the testimony:
God gave us eternal life,
and this life is in his Son.
Whoever possesses the Son has life;
whoever does not possess the Son of God does not have life.

I write these things to you so that you may know
that you have eternal life,
you who believe in the name of the Son of God.
The word of the Lord.

RESPONSORIAL PSALM

Ps 147:12-13, 14-15, 19-20

R. (12a) Praise the Lord, Jerusalem.
or:
R. Alleluia.

Glorify the LORD, O Jerusalem;
praise your God, O Zion.
For he has strengthened the bars of your gates;
he has blessed your children within you.

R. Praise the Lord, Jerusalem.
or:
R. Alleluia.

He has granted peace in your borders;
with the best of wheat he fills you.
He sends forth his command to the earth;
swiftly runs his word!

R. Praise the Lord, Jerusalem.
or:
R. Alleluia.

He has proclaimed his word to Jacob,
his statutes and his ordinances to Israel.
He has not done thus for any other nation;
his ordinances he has not made known to them. Alleluia.

R. Praise the Lord, Jerusalem.
or:
R. Alleluia.

GOSPEL

Lk 5:12-16

It happened that there was a man full of leprosy in one of the towns where Jesus was;
and when he saw Jesus,
he fell prostrate, pleaded with him, and said,
"Lord, if you wish, you can make me clean."
Jesus stretched out his hand, touched him, and said,
"I do will it. Be made clean."
And the leprosy left him immediately.
Then he ordered him not to tell anyone, but
"Go, show yourself to the priest and offer for your cleansing
what Moses prescribed; that will be proof for them."
The report about him spread all the more,
and great crowds assembled to listen to him
and to be cured of their ailments,
but he would withdraw to deserted places to pray.

Brothers and sisters, the Gospel of the Lord.

HOMILY:

During the medieval period, leprosy was considered a curse. Those afflicted were banished from the community, left to live in the fringes, separated by an unbridgeable chasm of fear and stigma. There is a tale of St. Francis of Assisi who, before his conversion, encountered a leper on the road. Repulsed by the sight and smell, St. Francis nevertheless mustered the courage to approach the man and kiss his hand. That act was a pivotal moment in the saint's life, an encounter with Christ in the guise of the leper. It crystallized for him what the Gospel demanded: love that goes beyond all barriers, even those erected by fear, prejudice, or disgust.

Dear brothers and sisters in Christ, as we read the Gospel of Luke (5:12-16) today, we are confronted with the profound story of a leper who approached Jesus, humbled but hopeful: "Lord, if you are willing, you can make me clean." And Jesus, filled with compassion, reached out His hand, touched him, and said, "I am willing; be clean."

We see in Jesus the God who wills our good, who desires our wholeness, who breaks every man-made barrier to reach us. Notice that Jesus touched the leper before healing him. He could have healed him with just a word, but He chose to touch him, to affirm his dignity, to banish his isolation even before banishing his disease.

In the leper's plea and in Jesus' compassionate touch, there are echoes of profound theological and existential truths. First, the leper's appeal to Jesus is rooted in a theological understanding that God is not distant, but immanent—ever willing to bend down to human suffering. Second, Jesus' gesture is the incarnate confirmation that no human condition could repel Divine Love. This is a love that dives deep into the grit and grime of human existence.

In a world that is increasingly isolating, where social, political, and even religious differences often cause us to keep at arm's length from one another, we must ask ourselves: Are we willing to be like Jesus? To touch and be touched, to heal and be healed? It challenges us to reconsider who the 'lepers' in our lives might be—the disregarded, the maligned, the voiceless—and how we can extend God's grace to them through our own compassion and action.

As we reflect on this Gospel, let us be inspired by the words of St. Augustine: "What does love look like? It has the hands to help others. It has the feet to hasten to the poor and needy. It has eyes to see misery and want. It has the ears to hear the sighs and sorrows of men. That is what love looks like."

In these challenging times, may we be emboldened by the Holy Spirit to reflect the compassionate touch of Christ to those most in need of healing, and in doing so, find our own spirits uplifted. Amen.

PRAYER:

Gracious and Loving Father,

We come before you today, your faithful gathered, stirred by the Gospel of Luke where we witnessed your Son, our Lord Jesus Christ, extend His merciful touch to the leper, a man marginalized and ostracized. As we bow our heads and lift our hearts, we are reminded that you are the God who heals, who restores, and who breaks down all barriers that keep us from fullness of life and from one another.

Lord, grant us the faith to come before you with our own wounds, whether visible or hidden, asking with humble hearts, "Lord, if you are willing, you can make me clean." May we never doubt your compassion and your deep desire for our wholeness.

We also pray, O Lord, for the grace to be imitators of Christ's kindness. Just as Jesus touched the leper, breaking the social and cultural bonds that held him captive, embolden us to reach out to the 'lepers' in our own communities—the forgotten, the rejected, and the misunderstood. Make our hearts places of sanctuary, our words echoes of your love, and our actions reflections of your boundless mercy.

Lastly, Father, we pray for those among us who are suffering physically, emotionally, or spiritually. May they feel your healing touch through our community, your Church, and may they find solace in the promise of eternal life through Jesus Christ, our Lord.

We offer these prayers in the name of Jesus, who lives and reigns with you and the unity of the Holy Spirit, One God, forever and ever. Amen.

JANUARY 12
SATURDAY AFTER EPIPHANY

READING 1

1 Jn 5:14-21

Beloved:
We have this confidence in him
that if we ask anything according to his will, he hears us.
And if we know that he hears us in regard to whatever we ask,
we know that what we have asked him for is ours.
If anyone sees his brother sinning, if the sin is not deadly,
he should pray to God and he will give him life.
This is only for those whose sin is not deadly.
There is such a thing as deadly sin,
about which I do not say that you should pray.
All wrongdoing is sin, but there is sin that is not deadly.

We know that anyone begotten by God does not sin;
but the one begotten by God he protects,
and the Evil One cannot touch him.
We know that we belong to God,
and the whole world is under the power of the Evil One.
We also know that the Son of God has come
and has given us discernment to know the one who is true.
And we are in the one who is true,
in his Son Jesus Christ.
He is the true God and eternal life.
Children, be on your guard against idols.

The word of the Lord.

RESPONSORIAL PSALM

Ps 149:1-2, 3-4, 5-6a and 9b

R. (see 4a) The Lord takes delight in his people.
or:
R. Alleluia.

Sing to the LORD a new song
of praise in the assembly of the faithful.
Let Israel be glad in their maker,
let the children of Zion rejoice in their king.

R. The Lord takes delight in his people.
or:
R. Alleluia.

Let them praise his name in the festive dance,
let them sing praise to him with timbrel and harp.
For the LORD loves his people,
and he adorns the lowly with victory.

R. The Lord takes delight in his people.
or:
R. Alleluia.

Let the faithful exult in glory;
let them sing for joy upon their couches;
Let the high praises of God be in their throats.
This is the glory of all his faithful. Alleluia.

R. The Lord takes delight in his people.
or:
R. Alleluia.

GOSPEL

Jn 3:22-30

Jesus and his disciples went into the region of Judea,
where he spent some time with them baptizing.
John was also baptizing in Aenon near Salim,
because there was an abundance of water there,
and people came to be baptized,
for John had not yet been imprisoned.
Now a dispute arose between the disciples of John and a Jew
about ceremonial washings.
So they came to John and said to him,
"Rabbi, the one who was with you across the Jordan,
to whom you testified,
here he is baptizing and everyone is coming to him."
John answered and said,
"No one can receive anything except what has been given from heaven.
You yourselves can testify that I said that I am not the Christ,
but that I was sent before him.
The one who has the bride is the bridegroom;
the best man, who stands and listens for him,
rejoices greatly at the bridegroom's voice.
So this joy of mine has been made complete.
He must increase; I must decrease."

Brothers and sisters, the Gospel of the Lord.

HOMILY:

Let us ponder for a moment on the remarkable humility of St. John the Baptist, a figure who parallels the focus of today's Gospel. It's often said that humility is not thinking less of yourself, but thinking of yourself less. There's a story of a renowned pianist who once played a concert for a small community. The local piano teacher was invited to come up and play something after the performance. The crowd whispered in disbelief, how could she dare to play after such a maestro? Yet, she played the same piece he had played, but with far less skill. Afterward, she received applause, not for her performance, but for her humility and courage. She said, "I can't match his skill, but we can both make music, and that is what's important."

My brothers and sisters in Christ,

As we delve into the Gospel of John today, we come face-to-face with a theological and spiritual lesson of profound magnitude—a lesson on humility and the understanding of our place in the Divine Plan. "He must increase; I must decrease," these are the words of St. John the Baptist. In a society obsessed with self-promotion and personal achievement, John stands out as a paradox.

As St. Augustine once said, "Humility is the foundation of all the other virtues; hence, in the soul in which this virtue does not exist there cannot be any other virtue except in mere appearance." Humility is not the degradation of oneself but the elevation of God and others. John was not void of personality, talent, or mission; rather, he had a clear sense of his role—preparing the way for the Lord. He understood that his importance was not diminished because Jesus had come; it was fulfilled.

John's life illuminates what it means to be a Christian, especially in our modern age. He was deeply rooted in reality, knowing both his purpose and his limitations. He was not the light but bore witness to the light, much like the moon reflects the light of the sun. In our lives, we are called to reflect the light of Christ, the true Sun, so that others may find their way to Him.

When we are filled with the Spirit of God, we understand that our joys, talents, and successes are not entirely our own, but shared achievements with the Divine. Our calling, then, is not to shine our own light but to reflect His. The light is less about us and more about the illumination it provides for others.

In this Eucharistic celebration, may we imbibe the humility of John the Baptist, to recognize that we are instruments in God's grand symphony, each with our own role to play. While we may not match the 'maestro,' we can still make music for God's glory.

May the words of John the Baptist echo in our hearts: "He must increase; I must decrease." And may we live this out, knowing that in making space for God to increase in our lives, we are not diminished but made complete. Amen.

PRAYER:

Heavenly Father, we come before You on this Saturday after Epiphany, humbled and grateful for the gift of Your Son, our Lord Jesus Christ—the light that dispels all darkness.

As we reflect on today's Gospel from John, we are reminded of the self-effacing wisdom of St. John the Baptist, who teaches us, "He must increase; I must decrease." Lord, grant us the grace to live this wisdom in our daily lives. May we always bear witness to the true Light, Your Son, and never let our egos obscure His radiant glory.

Father, as St. John the Baptist emptied himself to prepare the way for Jesus, we too ask for the strength to diminish our pride, our vanity, and our self-centeredness. Bestow upon us the spirit of humility, so that we may recognize the works of others, celebrate their achievements, and most importantly, magnify Your divine presence in our lives.

In a world that often promotes self over community, individual success over common good, and pride over humility, help us to be countercultural. May we be like St. John the Baptist, whose joy was made complete by the presence and prominence of Christ. Let our joy also be rooted in Your will and Your glory, rather than our own interests.

As we continue to journey through this season, keep us mindful of the sanctity and purpose of each moment. Help us to see that in allowing You to increase in us, we become the fullest versions of ourselves, reflecting Your grandeur and love to the world.

We make this prayer through Christ, our Lord, in unity with the Holy Spirit, one God, forever and ever. Amen.

CLOSSING PRAYER

Heavenly Father, as we come to the close of these spiritually enriching seasons of Advent and Christmas, we pause to offer our heartfelt thanks for the countless graces and blessings You have showered upon us. We thank You especially for the gift of Your Son, our Lord Jesus Christ, whose birth we have celebrated with joy and whose coming we anticipate with steadfast hope.

Lord, during Advent, You have called us to be vigilant and prepare our hearts for the arrival of the Savior. Through the Christmas season, You have reminded us of the indescribable love made manifest in the Word becoming flesh. Now, as these sacred seasons draw to an end, let not the fervor of our faith wane nor the light of Your love dim within us.

May the lessons of patience, expectation, love, and humility that we have gleaned from these holy times be integrated into the tapestry of our daily lives. We ask You, Father, to take these seeds of faith, water them with Your grace, and nurture them with Your wisdom, so they may bear fruits of righteousness, peace, and joy in the Holy Spirit.

Lord, as we prepare to step into Ordinary Time, help us to live extraordinary lives, inspired by the Nativity and guided by the teachings and examples of Your saints. We especially seek the intercession of the Blessed Virgin Mary and St. Joseph, whose obedience and faith were exemplary during the Advent and Christmas narratives.

Finally, Heavenly Father, bless our families, our communities, and our world with Your peace. Let the message of Advent be our rallying cry and the joy of Christmas our strength as we continue our pilgrim journey through this earthly life towards our eternal home.

We ask all of these things in the name of Your Son, our Lord Jesus Christ, who lives and reigns with You and the unity of the Holy Spirit, one God, forever and ever. Amen.

Father, I offer to you the goodness of my heart, the goodness of my soul and the goodness of my whole being. And Father help me to turn my vices into goodness through Christ our Lord our King and our Savior.

Amen

www.ingramcontent.com/pod-product-compliance
Lightning Source LLC
Chambersburg PA
CBHW070051080526
44586CB00013B/1006